"There is no word in the English language like the word *adventure*. *A Trip around the Sun* will awaken your hunger to make your life your adventure. If you can read this book without being stirred to life—check your pulse."

—John Ortberg, senior pastor of Menlo Park Presbyterian Church and author of *Soul Keeping*

"This is a terrific book, written by two of my favorite people on the planet. I've known Dick and Mark for many years, and they're trusted friends and guides. Though they are authors, scholars, leaders, and pastors, they don't care at all about titles. They care about people. I've seen the way they embrace the disenfranchised and the way they interact with leaders of entire countries. It's exactly the same. That's because they've learned to love people the way Jesus did. You'll want to do the same after reading this book."

—Bob Goff, attorney and author of *Love Does*

"A magnetic message of risk, reflection, and relationship. Throw this one in your luggage for your next trip around the sun."

—Christine Caine, author of *Unstoppable*

"This book will inform and inspire you during your annual trip around the sun. Writing from the overflow of remarkable living, Mark Batterson and Dick Foth provide an owner's manual for an abundant and adventurous life."

—Dr. Barry Black, Chaplain of the United States Senate

"Mark Batterson and mentor Richard Foth prove each trip around the sun deserves a healthy dose of adventure, risk, and relationship. With unique perspectives and a joint message, these two inspire their readers to 'risk more, reflect more, and do more things that live on after we die.'"

—Reggie Joiner, founder and CEO of Orange

"Shared life stories forge the chain of values that bind generations into cultures, then civilizations. As cultural DNA, these stories can be the 'good news' of human existence. When they mirror God's Word and God's Son, they are profound life road maps. For well over six decades, Dick has shared his life stories with me. For a score of years Mark has done the same, modeling devotion inspiring us to our highest and best. *A Trip around the Sun* is a trip well worth taking!"

—John Ashcroft, former US Attorney General

"This book will stir your soul! The stories that weave through life and the adventures that shape who we are with each other are brought to life in a tangible, real, practicable way that will enhance and inspire your trips around the sun."

—Curt Richardson, cofounder of OtterBox

"The synergy of Foth and Batterson is powerful. Everyone will find inspiration in these pages. As a father and grandfather I gleaned new ideas to involve my family in adventures that will bring them closer to Jesus."

—Rep. Frank Wolf, 10th District, Virginia

"Batterson and Foth bring together an enormous treasure of life experiences and biblical principles to guide us into the larger adventure of living our years to the fullest! Whether you are young, old, single, married, parenting, or teaching, *A Trip around the Sun* is a must-read and re-read. It challenges you not to settle for the safe seat on the bus but rather to think big, take risks, and periodically recalibrate your life compass."

—Barbara Melby, early childhood teacher

"I couldn't wait for the next chapter. I enjoyed it very much!"

—Tony Hall, ambassador and former US Congressman

"Dick and Mark have captured powerful stories and lessons for us as we search to find ways to sharpen our ability to walk in faith. Dick's friendship and connection overlapped my walk in service to our nation in challenging days—like the tragedy on the USS *Cole* and the attacks on 9/11—when I was looking to my faith for answers and direction. Together these gentlemen share some of the excitement and adventure and the love principles that change lives in our journeys 'around the sun.' This is a great read. It challenges us all in our walk with Jesus."

—Admiral Vern Clark, former Chief of Naval Operations, US Navy

"When two great communicators from two different generations collaborate on a book chronicling their adventures following Jesus, it's probably worth a look. Authors Mark Batterson and Dick Foth infuse warmth, disarming transparency, and insight into everything they do, and *A Trip around the Sun* is captivating and delightfully difficult to lay down. The gift of storytelling is in rare form here, and readers are invited into the authors' personal and professional journeys with moments from their mentoring friendship, vignettes from history, great quotes from some of history's great adventurers, and practical insights from God's Word. Everyday things become meaningful things, and generational perspectives engage us. No matter how many trips we've taken around the sun, Foth and Batterson whet our appetites to risk doing life with Jesus full-out, to do it with friends treasured and those yet to be made, and to leave a legacy of high adventure with God that will impact generations to follow. *A Trip around the Sun* is well worth the read!"

—Dr. Beth Grant, author of *Courageous Compassion* and cofounder of Project Rescue

A Trip around the Sun

Turning Your Everyday Life into the Adventure of a Lifetime

Mark Batterson and Richard Foth

with SUSANNA FOTH AUGHTMON

BakerBooks

a division of Baker Publishing Group
Grand Rapids, Michigan

© 2015 by Mark Batterson, Richard Foth, and Susanna Foth Aughtmon

Published by Baker Books
a division of Baker Publishing Group
P.O. Box 6287, Grand Rapids, MI 49516-6287
www.bakerbooks.com

Printed in the United States of America

Library of Congress Cataloging-in-Publication Data
Batterson, Mark.
    A trip around the sun : turning your everyday life into the adventure of a
lifetime / Mark Batterson and Richard Foth, with Susanna Foth Aughtmon.
        pages cm
    Includes bibliographical references.
    ISBN 978-0-8010-1683-7 (pbk.)
    1. Christian life. I. Title.
BV4501.3.B3877 2015
248.4—dc23   2014046399

Unless otherwise indicated, Scripture quotations are from the Holy Bible, New International Version®. NIV®. Copyright © 1973, 1978, 1984, 2011 by Biblica, Inc.™ Used by permission of Zondervan. All rights reserved worldwide. www.zondervan.com

Scripture quotations labeled ESV are from The Holy Bible, English Standard Version® (ESV®), copyright © 2001 by Crossway, a publishing ministry of Good News Publishers. Used by permission. All rights reserved. ESV Text Edition: 2007

Scripture quotations labeled KJV are from the King James Version of the Bible.

Scripture quotations labeled NKJV are from the New King James Version. Copyright © 1982 by Thomas Nelson, Inc. Used by permission. All rights reserved.

Scripture quotations labeled NLT are from the *Holy Bible*, New Living Translation, copyright © 1996, 2004, 2007 by Tyndale House Foundation. Used by permission of Tyndale House Publishers, Inc., Carol Stream, Illinois 60188. All rights reserved.

The authors are represented by The FEDD Agency, Inc.

15   16   17   18   19   20   21   8 7 6 5 4 3

To the ancestors who came before us—we're grateful.

To the generations who come after us—we're hopeful.

And to our wives, Ruth and Lora—
it wouldn't be half the adventure without you.

Contents

Introduction

Choose Adventure

Dick's Story

Walking down the West steps of the Capitol, I hunched my shoulders against the cold. The conversation I'd had with an old friend proved to be life changing. As I looked down the National Mall toward the Lincoln Memorial, the scene took my breath away. Golden rays of late afternoon sunlight softened the edges of the granite monuments and Smithsonian museum buildings, which frame the unique expanse that tells our nation's story. It made the line in "America the Beautiful" come alive: "Thine alabaster cities gleam." I still couldn't believe we were here. It was November 1994.

After fourteen years as president of a small private college in the Santa Cruz Mountains of California, I had come east with my wife, Ruth. We joined a cadre of friends working behind the scenes in Washington to be encouragers. The capital can be lonely for folks in power. Most people who want to be close to them want something in return. Inspired by others before us, we hoped to offer friendship with no strings attached and connect those who responded with each other in small clusters. In public life, small groups can be safer places. There individuals often blossom from the hope and support offered in the spirit of Jesus.

We were making friends and putting down roots during these cool autumn days. Thanksgiving was just around the corner. Having left our own grown children and extended family in California the year before to move to Washington, DC, we wanted and needed a "family fix." It also found us continuing the tradition we started with our family years before: *anyone without a place to go for the holidays was welcome at our table.* It made for good conversations and better desserts. This year we included Mark and Lora Batterson, a young couple who had moved from Chicago to Washington to work in the inner city. Though we were old enough to be their parents, we had one thing in common: *transition.* All of us were following a new dream.

Ruth and I had known Lora since she was a baby. Her father and mother, Bob and Karen Schmidgall, were gathering a congregation in Naperville, Illinois, around the time that Ruth and I were doing the same near the University of Illinois in Urbana. We connected with them immediately. Our friendship remained strong even after we left Illinois for California, almost twelve years later.

With that good history, looking out for their kids in Washington, DC, was a given. It was natural. To see Mark and Lora dreaming their own dream brought a thirty-year-long friendship full circle. We shared turkey and cobbler and laughter. We told stories and jokes. And ate more cobbler.

My friendship with Mark grew easily. When he and Lora felt called to form a congregation with what turned out to be nineteen people in an old school building in southeast DC, we chose to be two of the nineteen. It's great fun and a great pain to start something from scratch. Besides, when you are young and dreaming the dream, you need one or two graybeards around. If only for the money!

When I was a twenty-four-year-old greenhorn pastor in 1966, some people with a bunch of years on me changed my world. Paul and Eileen McGarvey were two of them. Paul was a football coach from a local high school and was fifteen years my senior. He would show up after two-a-day practices at the little building we were constructing and help me paint walls and actually make light fixtures. The lights looked quite good. Well, they looked good from twenty-five feet away. His presence and support of me, a stuttering young man from Oakland, California, made a huge difference. He showed me that he believed in me simply by showing up. Ruth and I wanted to be that kind of presence for Mark and Lora.

I invited Mark to join me at some of my breakfast meetings around town. We shared coffee and friends and talked about dreams. Mark went from being my friend Bob's son-in-law to being *my* friend. I watched as he found his own teaching style and began envisioning what National Community Church would someday become. I saw him blossom as a dad when Parker, Summer, and Josiah arrived. I saw him dream some pretty unique dreams and put feet to them. I watched him develop his gift for writing and flourish.

One day Mark walked me past a neighborhood crack house and said, "Wouldn't that be a cool place for a coffeehouse, just a block from Union Station?" A few years later we sat on that very spot drinking a latte at Ebenezer's coffeehouse. Within a couple of years it was voted the number one coffeehouse in Washington, DC.

To watch someone come into his own gives great pleasure. Mark is a Renaissance man in the best sense of the word. From his love for Scripture to his two-books-a-week reading addiction to his ease at taking pointers from old guys, he is a voracious learner. But he and I are quite different. He is a fine basketball player. That's not my game. He loves the Green Bay Packers. I grew up with the 49ers. He reads quantum physics to relax. I escape with Louis L'Amour. But the one thing that really connects us is *love of adventure*.

Adventure, by Google's definition, describes "an unusual and exciting, typically hazardous, experience or activity." It happens often without design and has a hint of chance about it. Whether it's identifying with the original adventure of Jesus coming to earth to unlock our world or us taking a risk in love, adventure is lifeblood.

In a fresh work venue, a trip to the heart of India, or a new friendship, adventure ripples just beneath the surface. We were meant for more than a safe ride when God placed us here. Any part of this life that offers more, requires more, or asks more of us than we are used to is an opportunity to grow more, dream more, and be more than we are now.

At the heart of it all is discovery. I have, so far, circled the sun more than seventy-three times. I have discovered a few things that matter: *Loving in the hard times is the best kind of loving. At the end of the day most folks do exactly what they want to, so we need to focus on the want to. Life is a wilderness, but when we invite Jesus to be our Guide, all bets are off.* Any way you slice it, those things spell adventure.

Twenty years ago I thought we were inviting Mark and Lora over for a little turkey and a lot of berry cobbler. Apparently, we were in for an adventure.

Mark's Story

When Lora and I moved to the nation's capital in May of 1994, we only knew one soul, my college roommate. Coming off a failed church plant in Chicago, we were looking for a second chance. So we packed all of our earthly belongings into a fifteen-foot U-Haul truck and moved to DC with no guaranteed salary and no place to live. Some would call that *foolish*. We chose to think of it as an *adventure*.

We found an apartment and started doing inner-city ministry. We poured ourselves into that ministry, but there wasn't anyone pouring into us. We felt like we were all by ourselves. At first that can actually be exciting, but it wasn't long until we felt downright lonely. Then Thanksgiving rolled around. It was our first major holiday on our own as a young married couple with no place to go. That's when the conspiracy happened. Dick and Ruth Foth were longtime friends of Lora's parents, Bob and Karen Schmidgall, and I think my in-laws were genuinely concerned about us being so far from home with no family and very few friends. So the Foths didn't just invite us over for a turkey; they took us under their wing.

Two things made an impression on me that Thanksgiving. The first was Ruth's mixed berry cobbler with Häagen-Dazs ice cream. I have a remarkable memory when it comes to food! The second was Dick's vast knowledge of trivial facts. If you're playing a game of Trivial Pursuit, Dick Foth is a first-round draft pick. I jokingly remind Dick now and then that he has more trivial knowledge than anyone I know! But his breadth of knowledge while playing Trivial Pursuit was what first revealed a holy curiosity about life that I have learned to love and admire about him.

Lora and I walked away from that one little encounter feeling loved and cared for. For me, love and care comes in the form of warm cobbler and high-quality ice cream. Little did I know that God would turn that meal into a lifelong friendship and mentorship.

My first service as pastor of National Community Church was held at J. R. Giddings Public School on January 7, 1996. Only three people showed up our first Sunday because of the infamous blizzard of '96: me, Lora, and our son Parker. The upside was that we experienced a 633 percent growth spurt the following Sunday. Dick and Ruth were two of the original nineteen attendees. They even brought a United States senator and his wife along for the ride. That made me a little nervous, but it also gave me a boost of confidence. It was a defining moment for me. Lora and I were just starting to dream this dream of planting a church in the nation's capital. We had no idea what it would look like or how it was going to turn out, but we knew the Foths were in our corner! Knowing that we had people who believed in us and were willing to dream with us made an incalculable difference at a critical stage of life and ministry.

I still remember my first sermon illustration that first Sunday.

Fifty people over the age of ninety-five were asked one question: *If you had your life to do over again, what would you do differently?* That's the perfect question to ask a group of people with five thousand years of cumulative life experience! Three answers emerged as a consensus: "We would risk more, reflect more, and do more things that live on after we die." After my message, the esteemed senator commented on that illustration, saying he really enjoyed it. What he didn't know was that it was about the only illustration I had. I had to go back to my sermon illustration books and borrow another one for week two!

While I didn't have much life experience at that point, I was hungry to learn. And I knew that Dick was someone from whom I could borrow a wealth of wisdom if he was willing to put it on loan to me. So Dick and I began to get together on a consistent basis. One of the most memorable meetings was lunch in the Senate dining room with the Chaplain of the United States Senate, Richard Halverson. The Senate dining room is only open to members of Congress, visiting dignitaries, and their guests, so it is a tremendous honor to be invited. You are rubbing shoulders with the who's who of Washington when you eat there. As we sat down for lunch, I could hardly concentrate on the menu because Muhammed Ali was seated directly behind us!

That lunch was par for the course. Dick Foth invited a twenty-six-year-old rookie pastor into his world. He shared his life, his faith, his wisdom, and his friends. And the reason is simple: *loving is sharing*. It's sharing your time, your money, your life, and your mixed berry cobbler. Dick Foth knows more things about more people than anyone I've ever met. He is a walking, talking encyclopedia of relationships. And it was his genuine interest in me that allowed me to share dreams and fears I'd never verbalized to anyone else. Dick became my sounding board. And his life will echo in my life forever—or maybe I should say, my life will echo his.

A few years into our church plant, Lora's dad died of a heart attack at the age of fifty-five. I lost not only a wonderful father-in-law but also my go-to guy for all my ministry-related questions. At my father-in-law's funeral, I stood at his casket and asked God for a double anointing. I wasn't even sure what I was asking for, but I knew I wanted to make a difference the way Bob Schmidgall had. I admired so many things about his life and ministry, and now he was gone. Virtually every situation I encountered in ministry was a new situation, a new challenge. I think the Lord allowed me, at an early age, to realize that if we try to fly solo, there is a good chance we'll crash land! I remember wrestling with a challenging situation one day and voicing my frustration to Lora about not having her dad to turn to anymore. Lora said, "Well, why don't you ask Foth?" So I did what all wise men do: I listened to my wife! It's no stretch to say my relationship with Dick helped me make some of my best decisions and kept me from making some of my worst. Dick became more than a mentor. He became a spiritual father and trusted friend.

More than anything, what has connected Dick and me these past eighteen years is our love of adventure. We both live by a simple mantra: *choose adventure*. We come at it from two different angles. I love a good challenge. He loves a good story. But both are born of adventuring.

There is a boyish quality about Dick that I admire. If I had to describe him in a single word, I would choose one of my favorite words: *neotenic*. It comes from *neoteny*, a zoological term that means *the retention of youthful qualities into adulthood*. Dick

15

is the youngest seventysomething I know! I recently spent two days with a life coach putting together a life plan because Foth told me I had to. He went through the same exercise the year before. Who puts together a life plan in their seventies? I'll tell you who: Dick Foth. And I'll tell you why: he's still not sure what he wants to be when he grows up! Dick is dreaming bigger dreams in his seventies than he was in his twenties. And I want to be around people like that. It's death-defying and life-giving.

Dick has shown me how to grow old and stay young at the same time. And I want to follow suit. In the words of Ashley Montagu, "I want to die young at a ripe old age."[1] That's more than a personal aspiration. That's a biblical command. In God's kingdom, childlikeness ranks right next to Christlikeness. Becoming more and more like a child is the true mark of spiritual maturity.

It's said that Teddy Roosevelt, my favorite president, would often be seen chasing his kids around the White House playing games. He'd keep heads of state waiting while he finished up a good game of hide-and-seek. That youthful zeal is something Dick embodies. His adventurous spirit is contagious. And I think that boyishness is in keeping with something Jesus said: "Unless you become like little children, you can't enter the kingdom of heaven."[2] Kids get adventure. It's innate. They live life free of worry, full of faith, and with their eyes peeled for the next big adventure. We should live with a holy anticipation of what's around the corner. Whether it's training to swim the Escape from Alcatraz with my daughter, Summer; hiking the Inca Trail with my son Parker; a week-long rafting trip through the Grand Canyon with Josiah; or a Play and Pray retreat with our staff, I am always looking forward to my next adventure. When you see life as an adventure, your hopes and dreams are never more than a day away!

One of the lessons I've learned from Dick is that adventure begs for company. When I was in my twenties, most of my goals revolved around my own personal development. But as I've taken more trips around the sun, I am trending toward togetherness. Almost all of my life goals—and I list 113 of them in *The Circle Maker*—have a relational component to them. I spent a magical day on Catalina Island, just off the coast of southern California, a number of years ago and fell in love with it. But I was there all by myself. I kept thinking, *I wish Lora were here.* So one of my life goals is to go back to Catalina *with* Lora. The first triathlon I ran by myself was certainly an adrenaline rush, but it doesn't compare to crossing the finish line with Parker when he was thirteen years old. I have reoriented almost all of my life goals so they involve someone besides me, because I don't want to cross the finish line by myself.

When you rise to the challenge of adventurous living, your days will be richer and your soul will be fuller. There will be more risks, more dares, and more obstacles. And in return, there will be more memories that started out as dreams. Adventure doesn't happen by accident. It has to be intentional.

I once wrote a magazine article titled "Get a Life."[3] It was an exhortation to my tribe, pastors. I have a theory: if your sermons are boring, it's probably because your life is boring! You have to *get a life* outside the four walls of the church so you actually have something to say that people can identify with. If you want to preach more interesting sermons, live a more adventurous life! And that exhortation isn't just for preachers. It doesn't matter who you are or what you do: *your life is your sermon.* To take it a step further, your life is a unique translation of Scripture. I'm the MAB version. Dick is the RBF. You may be the only Bible some people ever read. So the question is: *Are you a good translation?*

In John 10:10, Jesus said, "I came that they may have life and have it abundantly" (ESV). Do other people look at your life and want what you have? Or do they want no part of it? The abundant life Jesus offers is two-dimensional: quantitative and qualitative. By quantitative, I mean *eternal* life. It's the definition of "happily ever after." By qualitative, I mean an *adventurous* life—a life that is anything but boring. That was God's original intent when He created humankind. When God finished creating the heavens and the earth, He told His image bearers to take dominion over it. It was an invitation to explore every square inch of planet Earth. That certainly doesn't mean you have to be an oceanographer or astronaut to fulfill that Genesis commission. The greatest adventures aren't halfway around the world. They are often right across the street, down the hall, or in the seat next to you. You don't have to go looking for adventure. If you follow Jesus, adventure comes looking for you. Jesus didn't carry a cross to Calvary so that we could live a halfway life. He died so that we could come alive in the truest and fullest sense of the word.

I have made forty-four trips around the sun, at this writing. And I can't wait for the next forty-four, Lord willing. I want to live my life with a childlike sense of adventure. I want to leave a legacy that is full of faith and full of fun. And I know that the greatest adventures are always done in tandem with the people you love the most. So I will spend my days dreaming big dreams and praying bold prayers. I want to live out my first sermon illustration. Like those who had taken ninety-five trips around the sun, I want to risk more, reflect more, and do more things that live on after I die.

Will you join us?

Choose Adventure

1

For the Love of Risk

June 10, 1945. Fifth Avenue, New York City. A gigantic roar lifted to the skies as ticker tape filled the air. People began to shout, "There he is! Here he comes!"

In short pants and waving a small American flag, I was held by my dad in a crowd of shouting New Yorkers. The day was bright and the air electric. People flooded the sidewalks like ants, spilling down surrounding streets. Their cheers rose and fell like the roiling waves of the Atlantic. The tides of World War II had turned, and a beachhead of peace had been established in Europe. Radios and newspapers trumpeted the news that Germany and its great tyrant, Hitler, had fallen to the push of the Allies and a treaty had been signed. The troops in Europe were coming home.

Glistening horses ridden by New York's finest in dress blues cantered past us. Suddenly, there he was. General Dwight David Eisenhower, Allied Supreme Commander in Europe, swept by standing tall in the back of a gray convertible, grinning famously and waving with abandon to screaming crowds. That powerful image stays with me to this day.

Fast-forward a few weeks to the salt-sprayed decks of the SS *Gripsholm*, a Swedish ocean liner. I was a three-year-old on a journey by sea to India with my missionary-educator parents and sister. We had just dropped anchor in Naples, Italy. When chased out, the Nazis had blown up the harbor facilities. Bombed-out storage areas pocked the view, as did the shattered prows of sunken ships that pierced the surface of the harbor like tombstones in a watery graveyard. But I don't remember being scared. The briny scent of seawater filled my nose and the thrum of the ship engine vibrating beneath my feet translated to one thing: adventure!

That sense rocketed when we docked in Bombay, India. We stepped onto the pier to a cacophony of languages like Hindi and Gujarati and Malayalam swirling around us like a thick soup of pitch and intonation. The stifling heat sent sweat snaking down our backs and legs. The smells of spice and tea and people filled the air.

This was the land of Gandhi and Tagore, the beggar and the maharajah, the Bengal tiger and the king cobra. India assailed the senses. It was adventure with a zillion colors, sounds, and scents. For the next four years we lived in the far south of this subcontinent. Three of those years, my sister and I would board a cog railway steam train that would chug six thousand feet up into the manicured tea plantations of the Nilgiri Hills. Our destination? A British boarding school called Hebron. I came to know British education with all of its disciplines and rote learning against a backdrop of intense poverty, transcendent beauty, and now and again the sound of drums, cymbals, and flutes that signaled Hindu festivals in the nearby town.

Today they have an acronym for my kind of experience. It is TCK, for "third culture kid." That's a child who is introduced to a culture other than his parents' at an early age. Those cultures blend together to create a third culture. What was not my native home greatly influenced the native me. Ecclesiastes says, "A threefold cord is not quickly broken."[1] That refers to the strength people get from standing together, working hand in hand, not being alone. I think one of my threefold cords is cultural: American, British, and Indian. These are not equal cords, but they are real and they are mine.

The southern writer William Faulkner wrote, "The past is never dead. It's not even past."[2] To this day when I walk into the condiment section of a supermarket and smell curry powder, I am in India. That olfactory connection happens in the blink of an eye. When I watch *Chariots of Fire* or *Downton Abbey*, the accents and the class system draw me in. I am there.

Tender roots nurtured in the soil of high excitement and new possibilities produce a plant with spreading leaves. I am shaped by the breadth of my early exposures and the depth of my experiences in those years. These memories have made me.

Each vivid picture seems to shout one thing: *I was made for an adventure*. Somewhere in my DNA is a strand labeled "Foth Adventure." No doubt it's a combination of genetics and those first encounters with decidedly different cultures, but I see life as a grand escapade. New opportunities and new friends are always just around the corner. Tomorrow's outcome will be better than today's. Life brims with possibilities and is crammed with discovery. So a trip around the sun can be 365 days of unabashed adventure.

I wonder if Abraham felt that way when he obeyed and went to a land he did not know.[3] Or Jesus on the run to Egypt at age two with his parents trying to escape a vengeful Herod.[4] Or Moses, a Hebrew kid, found in a reed basket in the Nile by an Egyptian princess and ultimately brought up in the royal household.[5]

I have come to believe that from the moment of conception, we are being formed with an adventure in mind. We were created to touch, taste, smell, see, and hear life. Our Creator has big plans for us. No settling for mediocrity. Rather, we have a high calling etched into our bones and written on our hearts.

God wants to engage us from first squall to last drawn breath and deliver us into a life He has dreamed for us. Whether our earliest memories are sailing the high seas in a steamship or walking into a kindergarten class by ourselves for the first time, the exploration of the world within us and around us is a drumbeat. And the beat goes on.

We were made to explore. For some of us that exploration is more outward than inward, like Admiral Peary going to the North Pole. For others it is more inward than outward, like Pascal and his thoughts or Thomas Merton's contemplations. Whichever it is, we were made for curiosity and more. That design drives us. It shapes our thinking and our dreams. It forms expectations of what life should be and lays the foundation of who we will become. It shapes our destiny.

I would submit it *is* our destiny. When I met twenty-four-year-old Mark Batterson in 1994, I met a kindred spirit. We had very different roots but a common way of thinking. I knew hardly anything about him, but I sensed a possibility that something good was going on. Little did I know.

Mark's Story

Alfred Adler, the famed psychologist, is said to have begun every counseling session by asking his clients to tell him about their earliest memory. They would share those memories, and no matter what their answer was, Adler would say, "And so life is." If your earliest memory is flying in an airplane to visit your grandparents, life is a journey. If your first recollection is huddling under the covers on a summer's night as thunder claps and lightning strikes, life is a storm.

I have a theory: 87.2 percent of how we think about ourselves can be traced back to a few pivotal experiences. All right, I made that percentage up. But I genuinely believe our outlook on life is determined by a few defining moments when God meets us and we meet God. It's Jacob's wrestling match with God. It's Moses at the burning bush. It's Jonah in the belly of the whale. It's Peter walking on water. Those moments are more than memories from the past. They are spiritual astigmatisms. They are the lenses through which we perceive the present and dream of the future. Those are the moments when God helps us see ourselves for who we really are.

One of my earliest memories took place when I was four years old. I used to borrow a bike from my friend down the street, with or without his permission. One day he got tired of it. He marched down to my house and said, "You can't borrow my bike anymore."

"Why not?" I asked.

"Because my dad took off the training wheels so you can't ride it!" He had a triumphant look in his eye. So I marched down to his house and got on his bike. In the short ride back to my house, I learned how to ride without training wheels. I parked it in my driveway and put down the kickstand. Then I had a triumphant look in my eye! That is how I am wired. Tell me to do something and I'm unmotivated. Tell me it can't be done and I will die trying to do it. And I'll love every minute of it. Where is the joy in achieving something that is humanly possible? Give me insurmountable odds and I'm hooked. Life is a dare. And so life is, as Alfred Adler would say.

Not much has changed in the four decades since that first two-wheeled ride down my block. When you tell me something

23

is impossible, you are handing me a fast pass to my next great adventure. Tell me no and I will start looking for the yes. It doesn't matter whether it's paragliding over the Sacred Valley in Peru, hiking the Grand Canyon rim to rim, or biking a century. I love a challenge! Minimum risk equals minimum satisfaction. Maximum improbability equals maximum possibility.

I think my love of risk taking was passed down to me through my maternal lineage. My grandpa on my mom's side, Elmer Johnson, was an adventurer extraordinaire. It's best evidenced occupationally. He was elected the first municipal judge of Fridley, Minnesota. He and my grandma owned and operated an A&W Root Beer stand. And he was a professor at Northwestern Bible College in Minneapolis, Minnesota, during Billy Graham's brief tenure as president. In fact, one of the prized pictures in our family photo album is a snapshot of Billy Graham with a nylon stocking over his head at a faculty party that my grandparents hosted. I have no idea what kind of game they were playing, but my grandfather was fun loving. He had a keen sense of humor and an even keener love of life. He took God seriously, but he didn't take himself seriously. And that enabled him to walk to the beat of his own drum.

While he was a professor at the University of Minnesota in the 1960s, my grandfather included the whole family in his adventuring. In the summer months the family would pack up the car and drive into the Deep South to collect student loans. In a time of great racial segregation, he would often take the family to visit black churches on Sundays. He felt as comfortable in these congregations as in his own church. He even gave an impromptu testimony a time or two. Cultural norms didn't dictate his ability to engage and appreciate the world around him.

Every family has its own folklore—stories that are larger than life, stories that take on a life of their own. One of those stories in our family is how my grandfather started wearing a flannel shirt to Sunday night services when a suit and tie was the order of the day. My grandfather was criticized for it, especially because he was a deacon. But he felt like he could worship God better if he had a comfortable shirt on. Makes sense to me! I'm not sure what gene was responsible for that fashion decision, but whatever it was, I inherited it. If I'm wearing a suit, you can be fairly certain I am about to marry someone or bury someone!

I remember visiting my grandparents' home on the Mississippi River as a young child and being enthralled. Next to his love of adventure, my grandfather loved history. One of his prized possessions was a rare collection of dinosaur fossils. And there was one rule in my grandparents' home: *don't touch the fossils!* They were the tree of the knowledge of good and evil. To a five-year-old boy, they were also mysterious and alluring. If you recall, my life tends to be played out in terms of daring. And on more than one occasion this has gotten me into a little bit of trouble. I picked up one of these priceless fossils thinking, *No harm, no foul.* Then it slipped out of my five-year-old hands, fell onto the floor, and cracked in two. I'll never forget the sense of foreboding that washed over me as my grandfather walked in and assessed the situation. He didn't say anything. He just picked me up and held me close. Without using any words, he told me loud and clear: *Mark, you are far more valuable to me as my grandson than a dinosaur fossil could ever be.* The foreboding was replaced by an overwhelming sense of being loved. It was my first glimpse of amazing grace. I saw the power of what happens when someone loves you when you least expect it and least deserve it. It's life changing. It's life-giving. That kind of grace sets you free from past guilt and future fear. It allows you to experience the present as a *present*—a gift from God.

These two memories anchor my childhood recollections: a moment of adrenaline-pumping daring and a sense of all-encompassing grace. Risk taking and forgiveness. Experimenting and hope giving. It is the double helix of adventure that runs throughout my life and my ministry. A great adventure can shape your destiny. A bike ride without training wheels unleashed the risk taker in me. A grandfather's hug grounded me in grace. Each set me on a path of freedom—the freedom to be me. Each opened a new door—the door to adventure.

You are hardwired for an adventure that is as unique as you are. You may think that you are not an adventurer. You may never stand on the deck of an ocean liner and feel the salt spray on your face or face down the great chasm of the Grand Canyon on a rim-to-rim hike. But we are all wired for the ultimate adventure of following Jesus. When Jesus called the disciples to follow Him, the average person in the first century never traveled outside a thirty-mile radius of their birthplace. These men were planning on living their entire lives fishing the Sea of Galilee, but Jesus sent them to the ends of the earth. He took them adventuring with Him—they hiked the Mount of Transfiguration, sailed the Sea of Galilee, and went on long camping trips. Along the way, they witnessed remarkable miracles on a regular basis. And they did more than witness them. They filleted the miraculous catch of fish and ate it. They toasted the water that Jesus turned into wine and then drank it to the dregs. They hugged Lazarus while he still had his graveclothes on. You can't put a price tag on those kind of experiences, but once you've had them, they define you forever.

The very nature of the gospel is Jesus inviting the disciples on an adventure. To do what they'd never done and go where they'd never gone. Never a dull moment! You cannot follow Jesus and be bored at the same time. Søren Kierkegaard, the nineteenth-century Danish theologian, went so far as to say, "Boredom is the root of all evil." Boredom isn't just boring. It's wrong.

No one knows how many trips around the sun God will give them, but Jesus is calling you to the same adventure as

His original disciples. He is offering you a life full of daring. Don't you want in on the action? The moment you say yes, the adventure begins.

And so life is.

When You Follow Jesus, All Bets Are Off

2

Accumulate Experiences

The picturesque Charles River winds its way through rural Massachusetts and empties into Boston Harbor. Harvard, Boston University, and MIT all find their homes along its historic banks, and its waters are home to the Head of the Charles Regatta. On a hot summer's day the river teems with sculling crews and taut white sails of tacking boats.

The summer of 1983 found Ruth and me and our four kids sitting on a picnic blanket on the grassy banks of the Charles as night fell. We were not alone. We were one family in a crush of 250,000 who had come to celebrate the Fourth of July on the Charles River Esplanade.

The humidity of the day eased as a cool breeze came off the water. Hemmed in by picnic blankets and ice chests, weekend revelers and college students, we listened, enraptured, as the first notes of "The Star-Spangled Banner" filled the summer night. At our backs John Williams led the Boston Pops orchestra in a breathtaking rendition of our national anthem from the stage of the Hatch Shell. Our new friends the Coreys, native Bostonians and fellow adventurers, were introducing us to the Fourth of July, East Coast style. We delighted in the stirring pomp of Independence Day in a city so rich in history.

Song sheets for singing and trash bags for cleanup had been passed out as we entered the Esplanade. We lifted our voices with thousands of others at the swell of the violins. A lady to our right assumed an operatic stance, planting her feet on the grassy knoll, belting out the high notes like she was giving a professional performance. In a few minutes, as the *1812 Overture* reached a crescendo, fireworks screamed into the night sky and blossomed like a million purple and green and red stars above our heads. The reflected bursts of color on the water, the yachts and sailboats strung with lights, the thunder of the explosives, and the looks of wonder on our children's faces are things I will never forget. Those are things that can't be bought. The gift of experience is priceless.

Over the next few days, Hugh and Esther Corey and their family showed us the richness of a Massachusetts summer. Exploring the stalls of Faneuil Hall's circa-1742 marketplace. Bodysurfing in the warm coastal waters off of Cape Cod. Tasting butter-dipped lobster brought in fresh from the Atlantic and the fried crispiness of a New England hush puppy. Discovering the proper Bostonian pronunciation of a chocolatey fudgesicle ("fudge-ickle"). Each day was better than the last.

Ruth and I decided early on in our marriage that if we had to choose between giving our kids *experiences* or *things*, we would give them experiences. They could always get things. One of the ways we did that was by traveling. We didn't let modest salaries stop us. We packed food and games and stopped now and again just to play. After all, experiences connected to play are so often how we learn. I didn't intellectually know that at the time, but I learned it later and I know it's true. It's at the heart of who we are as human beings.

Stuart Brown, a medical doctor, psychiatrist, and founder of the National Institute for Play, says that *play, not necessity, is the mother of invention.* And play is not just for kids. He reports:

> A study done in Okinawa, Japan, by the National Geographic Society revealed that engaging in activities, like playing with young children, was as important as diet and exercise in fostering the Okinawans' legendary longevity. . . . When we stop playing, we stop developing, and when that happens, the laws of entropy take over—things fall apart. . . . When we stop playing, we start dying.[1]

It was an invitation to speak at a men's conference that had taken us east. It was also the summer before our eldest child, Erica, graduated from high school, so we took it as an invite to adventure. The conference took place over one weekend, and we morphed it into a month-long journey. Twenty-eight of those thirty nights were spent in the homes of friends, sleeping in guest bedrooms and on floors and pull-out couches. This is what we like to call "creative mooching." We creatively mooched our way down the East Coast!

We walked Boston's Freedom Trail and saw where the lantern was hung in the Old North Church for Paul Revere's midnight ride. We stayed at a bed and breakfast in Vermont that had once housed Norman Rockwell's studio, and we swung on a rope swing over his creek. We fished the Outer Banks of Cape Hatteras and watched a reenactment of England's first settlement on Roanoke Island, called *The Lost Colony*.

Those thirty days of adventuring birthed irreplaceable memories, copious amounts of laughter, relationships that flourish to this day, and a love for history that has been passed on to our kids. Our second daughter, Jenny, fell in love with Boston and returned in her post-college years to attend Gordon-Conwell Theological Seminary. Barry, the Coreys' son, became the president of Biola University and remains a close friend and colleague. We rarely eat a "fudge-ickle" without thinking of him. That summer is lodged in the memories of our children as "the summer." We lived life to the full and then some.

Years later Barry and his wife, Paula, and their three children moved from Boston to Los Angeles. Paula and the younger children flew to California. Barry did the experience thing with his fourteen-year-old son, Anders, through a male bonding road trip. Driving an aging Volvo and attired in shorts and Danish clogs, they set off with a simple set of guidelines: watch a minor or major league baseball game live as often as possible en route, and never eat in a chain restaurant. What a time they had. The Volvo-and-clog combo had to shrug off some raised eyebrows while attending a stock car race at Route 66 Motor Speedway in Amarillo, Texas. Outside of that, they were good.

Who knows what dreams can take root in your children's hearts when you choose to live your life adventuring? Who can fathom what new hopes will be born when you choose to experience life instead of just get through it? What relationships will be formed and continue to grow and flourish throughout their lives? How do you quantify the impact of exposing your children to history, relationship, and good food all in one shot? How do you quantify the impact it has on all of you?

Both Jesus and Paul call us to experiences. It intrigues me that Jesus spent so much time eating with people. It stuns me that he was executed because he ate with the wrong ones. Luke records the displeasure of the Pharisees:

> Then Levi held a great banquet for Jesus at his house, and a large crowd of tax collectors and others were eating with them. But

the Pharisees and the teachers of the law who belonged to their sect complained to his disciples, "Why do you eat and drink with tax collectors and sinners?"

Jesus answered them, "It is not the healthy who need a doctor, but the sick. I have not come to call the righteous, but sinners to repentance."[2]

And as structured as the apostle Paul is with his forensic and legal language, when it comes to his dreams, he puts them in experience language:

I want to know Christ—yes, to know the power of his resurrection and participation in his sufferings, becoming like him in his death, and so, somehow, attaining to the resurrection from the dead.[3]

Our experiences shape the way we think, the way we interact with each other, and the way we live. They add richness and depth and meaning to our days. You can give your children toys today that quickly end up in tomorrow's trash. Or you can deliver a living, breathing experience that shapes their souls, enriches their lives, and makes their world and yours a doorway to tomorrow. A day spent exploring the woods behind your house, a weekend sharing stories and homemade breakfasts with grandparents, or an out-of-town vacation spent visiting your college roommate's family can impact them for the rest of their lives.

When I think of all the unique things that Mark has done and wants to do, I am inspired. It makes me want to be forty-four again and take another run at it. I'd pay attention more. I'd think more strategically. He has helped me by the way he thinks intentionally about experience and play.

We don't know the number of trips around the sun we get to enjoy. Only God knows. But to saturate those trips with people and places, moments and memories, creates a richness that never stops. It allows the question "Remember when . . . ?" to fire the joy all over again.

Mark's Story

In his adventurous memoir, *A Touch of Wonder*, Arthur Gordon shares one of the defining moments of his childhood. When he was a small boy, his family spent their summers at a seaside cottage. Late one night, after Arthur had fallen asleep, his father came into his room, picked him up out of bed, and carried him down to the beach. Then he told Arthur to look up into the night sky and watch. Just as his father said it, a shooting star streaked across the sky. Then another. And another. Arthur's father explained that on certain nights in August, the sky would put on its own fireworks display. Six decades later, it ranks as one of Arthur Gordon's happiest remembrances.[4]

Reflecting on the influence of his father, Gordon said his dad believed that a new experience was more important for a small boy than an unbroken night of sleep. In Gordon's words, "I had the usual quota of playthings, but these are forgotten now. What I remember is the night the stars fell, the day we rode in a caboose, the time we tried to skin the alligator, the telegraph we made that really worked."[5]

What will your kids remember from their childhood?

I'll give you a hint: it won't be the things you purchased for them. It will be the things you did with them. And it probably won't be the things you preplanned as a parent. It will be the improvisational moments that can only be identified by a parent's sixth sense. If you capitalize on those moments, you'll make the same kind of impression on your kids as Arthur Gordon's dad did on him.

Arthur Gordon captured the essence of his father's ability to make memories this way: "My father had, to a marvelous degree, the gift of opening doors for his children, of leading them into areas of splendid newness. This, surely, is the most valuable legacy we can pass on to the next generation: not money, not houses, or heirlooms, but a capacity for wonder and gratitude, a sense of aliveness and joy."[6]

I want to be the kind of dad who opens doors for my kids. I want to feed their curiosity and spark their sense of adventure. And the opportunities to do so present themselves all the time. We simply need to train ourselves to see them and seize them.

Our lives are not just measured in minutes. They are measured in moments—moments when the minutes stand still. And it's those defining moments that define our lives! Life becomes an adventure when we start seeing the miraculous in the mundane. When we put feet to our passion or bear-hug a new challenge, it changes our outlook on life.

I recently spent an unforgettable weekend with my friend Bob Goff. For the record, it was Foth who first introduced us. Surprise, surprise! Bob Goff may be the most whimsical person I know. He invited some friends to his lodge in Malibu. Not Malibu as in California. Malibu as in the middle of nowhere, Canada. It took us eight hours by boat to get there. But when we did, a flatbed boat with a fully uniformed marching band was waiting for us. There was even someone playing the bagpipes, complete with kilt. That set the tone for the weekend. When it was time to depart, Bob jumped off the dock fully clothed while waving good-bye. It's tradition.

Bob Goff is a moment maker.[7]

I want to be one too!

One of my passions is missions. Spreading the Good News of God's love overseas and domestically through financial giving is something that I believe in wholeheartedly. One of the first things we did in our first year as a fledgling church was write out a sacrificial check to missions. We didn't have a lot of money, but we wanted the money we had to count for something. When you give your money to something you believe in, it shows that you have skin in the game. But giving can be a cop-out for going. A passion for missions takes on a whole different sense of ownership when you leave your checkbook at home and get on a plane yourself.

May 27, 2005, ranks as one of the most memorable days of my life, and I learned a lesson that has defined my life ever since. It was the last day of our missions trip to Ethiopia. The date is stamped in my memory because it was one of the craziest days of my life. The adrenaline rush I experienced is unparalleled. After a week of intense ministry, our team journeyed into the wilderness of the Ethiopian outback. We got held up at gunpoint by shepherds with AK-47s, went swimming in a natural spring heated by a volcano, and did a game drive through Awash National Park—all in a day's adventure. We ended the day worshiping God around a campfire. That night, tucked away in my pup tent, I was journaling about the amazing day I had just experienced and I heard the still small voice of the Holy Spirit say, "Mark, don't accumulate possessions, accumulate experiences." That moment, in the middle of an African game park, reshaped the way I viewed life.

I think most of us spend most of our lives accumulating the wrong thing: possessions. And we end up possessed by our possessions! We don't own things. They own us. But I made a decision that night that I would accumulate experiences, and I've been doing it ever since. That two-word mantra—*accumulate experiences*—is my modus operandi. It frames my life. It also frames our family. Lora and I want our kids to get in on the action, and it's our job to engineer those experiences.

When Parker was six years old, I took him fishing at the Tidal Basin in the shadow of the Jefferson Memorial. Parker had never been fishing before, so I had to do everything for him. I baited the hook and cast the line. I watched the bobber and set the hook. Then, as the line began to tug, I reeled in the fish until it was just offshore. That's when I handed him the reel and grabbed my video camera so that I could capture him catching *his* first fish. The truth is, it was all me! I set Parker up. I engineered that experience. And that's part of my portfolio as a father. I orchestrate opportunities for my kids. And that's precisely what the heavenly Father does for us!

Ephesians 2:10 is one of my life verses: "We are his workmanship, created in Christ Jesus for good works, which God prepared beforehand" (ESV).

Paul is making reference to a Middle Eastern custom that was practiced in that day and age. When a king was embarking on a journey, his servants would leave a few days before him to make sure his travel would be safe and to take care of any problems before he arrived. They would prepare the way for the king. They were his secret service, his advance team. The heavenly Father flips this concept for us, His servants. Instead of servants taking care of their king, the King of Kings takes care of His servants. The picture painted in this passage is simply this: God is setting you up! He is in the business of strategically positioning us in the right place at the right time. And His angels are our advance team! Each trip around the sun has been carefully choreographed for us by the Creator of the universe. We just need to take His cues.

The heavenly Father is preparing good works in advance for His earthly children, and I get to follow His example. As a father, I have the strategic advantage of providing experiences for my kids. We parents are environmental engineers. We can create experiences that open our kids' eyes to the incredible world that surrounds them. We can orchestrate opportunities for them to grow spiritually and emotionally. We can open doors for them and expose them to an experience-rich life that shapes their minds and engages their interest. We can teach them how to embrace life and live it as an adventure.

I want to cultivate the adventure gene in my kids, and the key is intentionality. Parker and I hiked the Grand Canyon from rim to rim after a year of discipleship. That was intentional. Summer and I tried to swim from Alcatraz to the shore in the San Francisco Bay. While they canceled the race due to fog, it was still a great adventure that we experienced together. That was intentional. Josiah and I went to Super Bowl XLV together, sharing our love of hot dogs and the Green Bay Packers. That was intentional. Being my kids' advance man has been one of my greatest privileges as a dad. No price tag can be attached to the pleasure I take in enriching my children's lives with experiences. The joy is exponential.

Defining moments. Intentional strategies. Adventurous living. Most of us spend our trips around the sun accumulating the wrong things. Possessions are a dime a dozen. Experiences are the currency of a life well lived.

Don't Accumulate Possessions.
Accumulate Experiences.

3

The Original Adventure

Dick's Story

I stepped out of my office at Bethany College to head down the long, concrete stairway toward the gym. Another day in an intense and circuitous stint as president of a small college set in two-thousand-year-old redwoods near Monterey Bay. Who knew what the next twenty-four hours would bring? It was always like that.

So many meetings, so many constituencies, and so many days raising dollars for operations, buildings, endowment, and anything else that felt like it needed money. I looked everywhere. The thought was fleeting, but harvesting old-growth redwoods was apparently out!

Looking behind me, I noticed one of our basketball players coming my way—a tall, lean, African American kid with a basketball on his hip and a hard look on his face. He was a new student. We hadn't met.

It was a perfect chance to ask one of my favorite questions: "Where do you come from originally?" Whenever I asked students this question, whether they were a transfer from the neighboring community college or a new arrival in San Francisco on a red-eye flight from Mumbai, India, the answer was always a window into who they were.

Sticking out my hand, I introduced myself. "Hi, I'm Dick. What's your name?"

His grip was tentative as he said, "Eric."

"Nice to meet you, Eric. So, where are you from?"

He hesitantly answered, "Oakland."

His body language said, "Let's not do this." I was trying to get past one-word answers.

"Oakland? That's great. I'm from Oakland!"

His head popped up, surprise in his eyes. "You're not from Oakland."

"I am! Born in Alameda and brought up in Oakland."

"You're kiddin' me." He looked me over again. A small smile played at the corners of his mouth.

"Nope. Went to Horace Mann Elementary and Frick Junior High."

"Frick Junior High? Get out! I went to Frick!"

Now he was engaged, looking me full in the face with a wide grin.

"Yeah, I did!" I blurted. "We may be the only two guys who graduated from Frick who are still alive!"

His palm swung up in a reflex high five.

"Bruthah!"

The white forty-six-year-old college president in a three-piece suit and the black eighteen-year-old freshman in shorts and a sweatshirt were connected. We came from the same take-your-chance-on-the-street place. Five black fingers slapping five white fingers sealed the deal. He got it. I got it. We were good. We could begin our own adventure.

I was born in a maternity ward in the Navy town of Alameda, California, on St. Patrick's Day 1942, one hundred days after the Japanese attack on Pearl Harbor. From the fifth grade through high school, I lived in an 1100-square-foot bungalow on Congress Avenue in east Oakland, just three miles across the estuary from that maternity ward. My adult life took me to the cornfields of Illinois and the halls of power in Washington, DC, but my roots are found in the gritty urban soil of Oakland's East Bay. A shared birthplace or homeland can connect us with our fellows, like it did with Eric and me. But our real adventure begins when we connect to our Creator.

The problem is location. Real estate and kingdom business have that in common. Where things are located makes all the difference. He is the Holy One, the High Exalted One in heaven. And we, the unholy ones, are separated from Him, stuck here on a broken earth. There is no common ground. But the God who would do everything to have relationship with us fixed that. He bridged that gap when He chose to put on skin in the person of Jesus. He swapped His rightness for our wrongness, His access for our distance, an open door for relationship with the Father. He is our common ground.

Jesus came to us. He came to walk into the East Oaklands of our lives. But He didn't leave it there. When He invites us into relationship with Him, it changes our trajectory. This is where our journey begins.

New Testament scholar Dr. Gordon Fee said that life is a wilderness, and a compass doesn't help very much. A map certainly doesn't help because you have to know where you are for starters. What you need in a place you've never been before is a guide. Jesus becomes the Guide to the Father's house.

Years after that conversation with Eric, I moved to Washington. Starting to work with government and military leaders revolutionized the way I saw myself and my own journey of walking with Jesus through the wilderness. Growing up in the church, I had been shaped by events—church services, special speakers, and youth camps. That was fine, but on Capitol Hill there were no church potlucks, Easter musicals, or *kumbayahs* around a campfire. It came down to grappling with family issues over coffee with one or two friends, or a shared prayer spoken behind closed doors. It was discipleship boiled down to its essence. It was about journey.

In working through nonreligious language to explain that journey, the idea of place became very important. Jesus says, "Here's the deal! I'll leave My place. I'll come to your place. I'll take your place. And then we'll go to My place." This simplicity captured me. Everyone understands places. We all have them. It's where we live our lives day to day. Then Jesus walks into our place and redirects us.

It is not unlike Paul in Athens, when he goes to the place of dialogue, Mars Hill:

> Paul then stood up in the meeting of the Areopagus and said: "People of Athens! I see that in every way you are very religious. For as I walked around and looked carefully at your objects of worship, I even found an altar with this inscription: TO AN UNKNOWN GOD. So you are ignorant of the very thing you worship—and this is what I am going to proclaim to you."[1]

He sort of assumes the privilege of squatters' rights and camps in an open space. He sees an opening and takes it.

Jesus meets us where we are, in the crowded halls of Frick Junior High or the marbled halls of Capitol Hill. He says, "I've got a place for you. A new life. A new character. A new way of seeing things. How would you like to go on that adventure?" He joins us in our humanity, forgives all of our mistakes, and fills us with His hope. It's a win-win. I fulfill His dream for me, and He gives me some of my own.

Sometimes getting a clear view of Jesus is the greatest challenge. Time and distance can obscure Him and make Him institutional or insipid.

Dorothy Sayers, the British mystery writer and contemporary of C. S. Lewis, cuts through all that when she says,

> The people who hanged the Christ never, to do them justice, accused him of being a bore—on the contrary; they thought him too dynamic to be safe. It has been left for later generations to muffle up that shattering personality and surround him with an atmosphere of tedium. We have very efficiently pared the claws of the Lion of Judah, certified him "meek and mild," and recommended him as a fitting household pet for pale curates and pious old ladies.[2]

I don't want to muffle up that shattering personality. I want to revel in it. Then I want to reflect it.

When we go adventuring with Jesus, He takes us places we never dreamed we could go, gives us ideas we never thought we could have, and gives us friends that last forever. I have gotten all three of those pieces through my friendship with Mark. Always new places—I covet his trips to the Grand Canyon and the Galápagos Islands. Always new ideas—he's a brainiac with interests in almost any field. Always new friends—what a joy I've had working with his young and exciting team at National Community Church. It's a terrific experiential learning curve.

The journey with Jesus looks different for each of us, but the beauty of it is that we are headed for the same place. His place. Mark and I want to check it out.

Mark's Story

Jesus was the quintessential adventurer. Leaving the comfort of heaven, He entered the four dimensions of space and time He created and set out on the craziest adventure of them all: restoring broken image-bearers to Himself. He didn't do it with angel armies or legions of dedicated yes-men. He didn't overthrow the Roman government or claim the Kingship that was rightfully His. He was a middle-of-the-marketplace Messiah, who rubbed elbows with the masses. He hung out at wells and in living rooms and on hillsides and invited anyone and everyone to join Him. Jesus didn't come with an agenda; He was the agenda. He came that He might draw all men unto Himself. With His grace, with His truth, He lets us get in on the action with a life-altering invitation: "Come, follow me!"

Jesus' approach to living was revolutionary. The moment He stepped on this earth, He challenged the norms of society. When He said "the first shall be last and the last shall be first" in his kingdom,[3] He backed up His words with how He spent His days. He preferred the company of beggars, thieves, and blue-collar workers. Religiosity was out and relationship was in. Where the political leaders of the day were unapproachable, He made Himself absolutely accessible. Where the religious fathers practiced separatism and bigotry, He practiced familiarity and empathy.

When Jesus invites us to do life with Him, He invites us to rub elbows with those He loves—the lost, the broken, the misled, and the misfits. Just like Jesus, we need to find ourselves in the middle of the marketplace. If we are separating ourselves from the world around us, we are off mission. And even worse? We are missing out on the adventure Jesus has for us.

One of our three core convictions at National Community Church is that the church belongs in the middle of the marketplace. As our pastor of mission, Dave Schmidgall, likes to say, *a church that stays within its four walls isn't a church at all*. Paul didn't stand outside the Aereopagus and boycott. He went toe-to-toe with some of the greatest minds in the ancient world competing for the truth. In the words of Michelangelo, we need to *criticize by creating*. That doesn't mean creating our own subculture. It means writing better books, producing better films, and starting better businesses. Here's what I know for sure: you can't be the hands and feet of Jesus if you're sitting on the back of your lap. In too many instances, we've turned being a Jesus follower into a noun. Following Jesus is a verb. More specifically, an action verb. This year, NCC will go on thirty-three missions trips. In my opinion, one mission trip is worth more than a year's worth of sermons! Well, maybe not Foth's sermons. But mine for sure!

NCC was a ragtag group of about fifty members when the DC public school we were meeting in closed its doors. I'm embarrassed to admit it, but these are the words I journaled on that fateful day: "We've been backed into a corner." But in truth, God wasn't backing us into a corner. He was opening a door of opportunity. He was positioning us to be in the right place at the right time. God uprooted us from a run-down school on Capitol Hill and planted us in the movie theaters of Union Station. At the time, meeting in movie theaters for a church service was a rather novel concept, but it became part of our DNA.

For eighteen years, we've functioned more like a tabernacle than a temple. In the Old Testament, the temple was a stationary place of worship, and the tabernacle was mobile. Every time the cloud moved, people packed up their makeshift place of worship and moved with it. Movie theaters have been our tabernacles. Unpacking and repacking church every Sunday using Rubbermaid tubs isn't glamorous. We get our hands dirty week in and week out, but we wouldn't have it any other way. It doesn't allow us to forget that church is *not* a building. You can't go to church because you are the church.

The first Sunday we met at the theater, the movie posters in the theaters on either side of us read *Booty Call* and *Private*

Parts. We became quite gifted in the art of strategically placing artificial trees! And God began strategically placing us in the middle of our Capitol Hill community. Union Station is a hub of transportation for buses, trains, and the Metro in Washington, DC. You can't get more central than that. By placing us in such a pivotal location, God was making us both visible and accessible. Every Sunday as we worshiped, we intersected with tens of thousands of people who walked the halls of Union Station.

Over the last eighteen years we have seen that core value develop. We have gone from one church meeting in one location to one church meeting in seven locations. Seven theaters planted in the middle of thriving communities. Popcorn is our incense and ICEE drinks run in our veins. So when God moved upon our hearts to renovate a crack house near Union Station, it wasn't to build a church building but to build a coffeehouse—a place where our church and community could cross paths. Why? Because coffeehouses are modern-day wells. We've had more than a million customers walk through Ebenezer's doors! I doubt that would have happened if we had simply built a church building. And often one thing leads to another—we've seen many customers come to church and come to faith. I happen to believe that kingdom seeds bear a resemblance to coffee beans!

Where did this idea come from? Part of it is the way I'm wired. My greatest fear when I felt called to ministry was that I'd end up in a religious bubble. Frankly, that's the last place I want to be. But I also need to give credit where credit is due. Very early in our friendship, Dick shared with me some of the novel things he did as a young pastor in Urbana, Illinois. He had a radio talk show that aired right after Charles Osgood's *Newsbreak* on their local CBS affiliate. That was way outside the box in the early 1970s. Dick also would often send teams out door-to-door during Sunday morning services. He figured that's when people who don't go to church would be most likely to be home. Sending people away from meetings is a risky move for any pastor anywhere, anytime! Dick's example inspired me to take similar risks that made sense in our context. It also inspired one of our core values: *playing it safe is risky.*

Not having much money encourages you to risk. Foth wanted to take university students to Mexico during Christmas and Easter breaks to work with poor children in the slums, but how? In 1968, he and five friends signed a personal note for $2,500 to buy a 1948 GMC four-cylinder diesel bus from a transit company to start the Mexico trips. Not only did they have to learn how to drive the big rig, the reverse gear didn't always work, so students would pile out of the bus to push it backwards when necessary. Oh, and the heater didn't work. They traveled sitting up in sleeping bags that first Christmas because the temperature when they left Illinois was in the single digits.

That's often what adventure looks like. Of course, the students loved it. And I have a hunch the heavenly Father did too!

While I was in seminary, one seminal thought greatly impacted my philosophy of ministry. I believe it originates with renowned sociologist James Davison Hunter. During the last century, the church has reversed a significant sequence. In most churches today, you have to "believe before you belong." But going back into the annals of church history, this wasn't always the case. When you look at the Gospels, the disciples followed Jesus around for a long time before He popped the question, "Who do you say that I am?" Months of fish fries on the beach, cross-country treks, hillside teachings, miraculous healings, and cold nights camping out with Jesus led up to that question. They knew everything from His eating habits to His idiosyncrasies. They saw the playful side of His personality and the different way He interacted with Pharisees and prostitutes. They heard the authority in His voice when He threw out the money changers and cast out demons. They heard the tenderness in His voice when He blessed little children. With Jesus, it was about belonging first and believing second. The essence of who Jesus was had worked its way into the disciples' souls, a sort of spiritual osmosis, by the time Peter answered the question of who Jesus was. Countless hours spent in the presence of the Messiah prompted Peter to say, "You are the Son of the living God."[4]

Whether it is engaging folks at the counter of Ebenezer's coffeehouse or inviting friends to join us in community outreaches, we've tried to adopt that sequence, "belong before you believe," at National Community Church. We're about to break ground on a Dream Center in one of the toughest zip codes in DC. Why? Because that footprint gives us a foothold in a tough part of town. And that's how you break a stronghold.

Middle of the marketplace living means inviting people to join us in what we are doing before they know Whom we are doing it for and with. We've had a number of people come to faith in Christ because they've gone on a missions trip. We know that they aren't believers, but we let them belong. When they hang out with us, they see who Jesus is in the process. The Holy Spirit has a way of weaving the love of Jesus into the spirits of people even before they fully know Him.

One of the most profound lessons I've learned from Dick is this: if you're walking with Jesus and you invite someone to walk with you, there is a good chance they'll get to know Jesus somewhere along the way. It's a very simplistic perspective on evangelism, but it's very biblical. When Jesus walked and talked with the disciples along the road to Emmaus, He set an example for us to follow. We sometimes want people to cross the line of faith without having to walk with them, but most people don't even get to the starting line that way! In Dick's words, "When they get me, they get the Father, Son, and Holy Spirit." It's a package deal.

47

Our greatest adventure comes when we follow Jesus. When we do this, we find ourselves in the thick of real living. We frequent modern-day wells and talk to the person seated next to us on the Metro. We eat lunch with our co-workers and invite them over for bowls of ice cream. We pull weeds and paint houses in rough neighborhoods and ask our friends who don't know Jesus to be a part of revitalizing the community. What they don't know is that they are on the path of being revitalized themselves. After all, that's what Jesus does best.

When we are rubbing elbows with the masses, we are on mission. When we accept others where they are and show them the love of Jesus, we are revolutionary. And when we invite people to hang out with us, we get to see the metamorphosis of those who belong turn into a legacy of those who believe. It just doesn't get any better than that.

Criticize by Creating

4

The Preposition That Will Change Your Life

Dick's Story

A lot more happens in the United States Senate dining room than just eating. It is not unusual to see senators, congressional representatives, and the occasional celebrity chatting together over a bowl of the famous bean soup. But the ideas being talked about? That's where the action is.

I felt great excitement and some trepidation when my friend Richard Halverson, Chaplain of the Senate, asked me to lunch. I was awed by the stately room with its crystal chandeliers and those of note seated at the tables. The camaraderie and energy around the room was palpable.

I've always tried to play it cool when I am out of my element. In this room I was a small fish in a huge pond. It was clear that I was in a place where an impassioned pitch over a tuna salad sandwich could shape policy for a nation. Wondering how the chaplain interacted with this elite group of people, I asked him, "How do you work with senators?"

He pondered the question for a while before answering:

> My first pastorate was in Coalinga, California, out near oil fields in the center of the state. The congregation was mostly women who wanted to "get their husbands saved." These were business guys and oil riggers. They were busy fellows with full workloads. I had to go find them. Over my four years there, many of them started following Jesus.
>
> I found you have to do two things in working with business leaders: *you have to go where they are, and you have to respect their time,* because time is money. A fifteen-minute conversation or an early breakfast, as opposed to a lunch, was most beneficial in getting together. When I became chaplain, I decided I would meet a senator anywhere, anytime, under any circumstance, at his convenience, with no agenda. Except his.

My brain was cranking, taking in his words. "Yes," I said, "but you have an agenda. You want that guy to follow Jesus."

He smiled and said, "Oh, no, that's not my agenda. That's my life."

Dick Halverson continued to flesh out that thought with a practical premise. He told me that one preposition in Mark 3 was a game changer. After praying all night, Jesus chose the twelve to be *with* Him and preach the Good News and cast out demons.

> Jesus went up on a mountainside and called to him those he wanted, and they came to him. He appointed twelve that they might be with him and that he might send them out to preach and to have authority to drive out demons.[1]

That four-letter preposition *with* changed Dick Halverson's view of the Kingdom. The idea of coming alongside and working *with* and being *with* people as opposed to speaking *to* or *at* them changed everything for him. And his insights changed me.

More than that, Jesus simply calls me to be *with* Him. Being with someone is an entirely different paradigm than speaking *at* someone. The difference between pushing my agenda or just living my life determines whether a listener feels like a target or a friend. If in fact the Good News is embedded in us, as opposed to a cliché that we spout on occasion, the implications are monumental. Over the course of fifteen years in DC, I took Dick Halverson's words to heart.

One of the great delights of my years was the opportunity to have an aide-de-camp on occasion. That was a young male college graduate who worked with me for a year as driver, personal assistant, and colleague. In a place where parking is expensive or virtually nonexistent, a driver is extremely valuable. It is good stewardship of time. And, besides, it made me feel like a big shot!

We would spend many hours a week driving between appointments and being in meetings. Life issues were the order of the day. We talked about sports and God and food and women and sports and women and Scripture and women. You know, guy stuff. I had six aides over the years. They are now scattered around the country—a businessman in Boston, an Air Force chaplain, an IT executive, two pastors, and a president of an anti–human trafficking foundation. They taught me much. *With* goes both ways.

Although Mark was not an aide to me, the connection was every bit as real. To see how he has put together the team at National Community Church has been a delight. Each member of the team brings a gift, a spark, and a skill to the table. Whether they're traveling together, playing cornhole, or water-skiing, he's in the middle of the party. And the fact that they enjoy being together translates to this congregation that sprawls like mercury across the Washington metro area. Energy is never the issue because the median age of the congregation is twenty-eight, and more than 50 percent are single. Finding the time to engage is the issue.

In the world of relationships, *with* is not an add-on. This is not "coffee with cream" or "Do you want fries with that burger?" *With* is the Higgs boson "God particle" of relationship. The very idea is captured early on in Scripture when God says, "It is not good for the man to be alone."[2] Grafted into our bones is a need for each other. We are more complete with others. We are better when we are with them. If you want to really know me, you have to be around me when I am with my wife, Ruth. In her presence I am a better me. I have been transformed by her love over these past fifty years.

The names of God are a clear heads-up to us. He is Immanuel, God with us. He is the Paraclete, which means one who is called to the side of another. He is the Creator who commits to being with those He has created. When Jesus says, "I am with you always, even to the end of the age,"[3] He touches our core. The certainty and creativity that comes from His presence is stunning. When we spend time with Him and others spend time with us, the net result is that they spend time with Him. Matthew 10:40 says it best: "He who receives you receives Me, and he who receives Me receives Him who sent Me" (NKJV).

Time invested together is the best of temporal and the best of eternal relationship all at one shot. We should not then be surprised when what we think is an early morning breakfast with a colleague turns out to be way more than two eggs over easy. It becomes transforming.

Dick Halverson's insights about *with* flipped my theology inside out. Senators weren't the only ones speaking powerful ideas over lunch that day.

Mark's Story

My oldest son, Parker, is my soul mate when it comes to life-threatening adventures. If there is any chance of death, Parker is all over it. My daughter, Summer, would rather live! But she did agree to do the world-renowned Sharkfest Swim with me a few years ago. The swim covers 1.5 miles from the island of Alcatraz to the beach of San Francisco's Aquatic Park. We were hoping the Sharkfest part of the name was just a catchy slogan, but it's not. The waters are, in fact, shark infested.

When each of our children turns thirteen, I take them on an adventurous trip to celebrate their grand entrance into teenhood. The adventures don't have to involve man-eating carnivores, but Summer was up for the challenge. We trained during the winter months at our local pool and did a few practice swims in the Potomac River. On the morning of the race, the adrenaline was racing! We were geared up with wetsuits on, ready to jump into the 57-degree water. We actually couldn't see the shoreline because of thick fog, but that comes standard in San Francisco. This was going to be epic! Then, just before we jumped in, the event organizers announced over the bullhorn that the race was canceled due to the fog. At first I thought it was a joke, a bad joke. It wasn't. We had flown all the way across the country, and there was no backup plan. The collective letdown of eight hundred swimmers, some who had flown halfway around the world to be there, was visceral. At least we still got to eat the traditional post-race clam chowder. It took a while for the fog of disappointment to lift, but that letdown is now a memory that makes me smile. Like soldiers who are foxhole friends, Summer and I forged a bond that day. And that's what adventure does—it's like Gorilla Glue.

We came, we saw . . . we got sent home.

We had been through something both exhilarating and disappointing, and we had been through it together. Those kinds of memories that are shot through with the adrenaline of adventure hyperlink our hearts to the ones we experience them with. I would much rather experience life's adventures with someone than relay those adventures secondhand. But I haven't always been that way.

By nature, I'm more of an *intrapersonal* processer. I do some of my best thinking by myself. That's how I'm wired. But there has been a change in my life over the last ten years, and Dick has had a lot to do with that. He is an *interpersonal* processor. Dick always has someone with him, whether it's an aide-de-camp, a son-in-law, or a friend he's made in the last five minutes. He has shown me that doing life *with* other people makes it twice as good. Seeing how he lives his life in relationship has influenced me. I'm much more likely to invite someone along for the ride. If I'm traveling to speak somewhere, for example, I'll take a family member or staff member with me.

I love a good opening line. Of course, none equals Genesis 1:1: "In the beginning." Some classics include Melville's "Call me Ishmael" and Dickens's "It was the best of times, it was the worst of times." My personal favorite? It might be the opening line of *The Purpose Driven Life* by Rick Warren. It's so simply put: "It's not about you."[4] So simple yet so difficult.

One of the truths that Dick has helped me come to terms with is that *we* is greater than *me*. Life is miserable when it's all about me, myself, and I. Then *me* turned into *we* the day Lora and I got married. The *we* of marriage is complicated, but it has a way of doubling joy while dividing difficulties. Then we added to our *we* with Parker, Summer, and Josiah. Our energy was divided three ways, but our joy has tripled.

Then there is the *we* of church. God doesn't just give us a biological family. He gives us a spiritual family. Both of those families are dysfunctional, no doubt about it. But what a gift from our heavenly Father—not one family but two.

With isn't just a relational word; it's a God word. God Himself is *we*—Father, Son, and Holy Spirit. And He invites us to be part of His Great Commission. The key is *co*. It's God with us, in us, for us. In the process, *with* becomes a word you can stake your life on. Serious theological ramifications are packed into those four letters. Whenever I find myself struggling with something in my life, I have fallback positions. They are ramparts of truth that can steel me against what I am facing. When all else fails, one of the verses I hold on to is Jesus' promise, "I am with you always."[5] When my world seems to be turning upside down, that truth is the axis that keeps everything spinning. I only need to know two things: God is *with* me and God is *for* me. And with each trip around the sun, I believe it more and more.

If you have ever had someone in your life who is with you and for you, you won't likely forget it. It makes an imprint on your soul. My parents have always been my number one fans. If I were playing one-on-one with Michael Jordan, my mom would have placed bets on me!

One of the defining moments of my life happened as a freshman playing basketball at the University of Chicago. We had an away game at Brandeis University in Boston, and my parents drove all the way from Illinois to watch me play. That's right, they made the twelve-hour trip to watch me play for all of five minutes in the second half. Then they turned around and drove through the night to get back home. If I had to sum up what I appreciate most about my parents in a single phrase, it would be this: they were there for me. They were *with* me and *for* me. Their faith in me fueled my faith.

I think my earthly parents modeled what the heavenly Father is so good at—being with us and for us. He is our foxhole friend. He is the One who rushes in when everyone else runs away. He is the One who shows up in our lives when we need Him most and reminds us that He will never leave us or forsake us. If God is with us, we can make it through anything. If God is for us, it doesn't matter what comes against us. Without Him, we can do *nothing*. With Him, we can do all things. When we let God turn *me* into *we*, it is more than a paradigm shift; it is a life-altering phenomenon. It is the inflection point where a good adventure becomes a God adventure.

It Doesn't Matter What Comes against You If God Is for You

5

Who Is More Important Than What

Dick's Story

I had a deal with God. If I ever had to pastor, a role I perceived to be unbelievably boring, I wanted to be in a campus town. And it happened. We headed out from the orchards and vineyards of Modesto, California, to the tall corn of east central Illinois in the mid-1960s. We were on our way to pastor a group of a dozen students from the University of Illinois and three young professional couples.

With some years of trial and error, lots of prayer, and God's grace, that cluster of committed folks developed into a thriving congregation. The Jesus movement and the Vietnam War were going full bore. Campus riots and torched inner cities expressed the times. University students looking for real purpose and new life were running head-on into the love of Jesus and embracing Him with abandon. Being a young pastor in a college town in those years kept me running a mile a minute and was full of surprises. God was up to something, and we were getting to ride the wave.

One Sunday evening, we opened the microphone and asked for prayer needs from the congregation. One young guy, Jim, stood up and said, "I'd like to pray for Paul."

Paul was forty years Jim's senior. A former tank commander under General George Patton in the famous Fourth Armored Division at the Battle of the Bulge in World War II, Paul was a two-packs-a-day guy with emphysema and a lot of physical problems. I immediately wondered if his health had taken a dive.

"Is Paul in the hospital?"

"No."

"Is he sick at home?"

"No."

"Is he struggling with depression?"

"Not that I know of."

Perplexed, I asked, "Jim, why do you want to pray for him?"

He grinned at me and said, "Well, I just like him."

That answer will throw a pastor off. We like to reserve prayers for dire situations. You know, disease and tragedy. If you have cancer or have lost your home, you're on the list. But you can't just pray for your friends for no reason. You can't just pray for people you like!

Liking is an interesting motif. One of the results of our twelve years in Illinois was friendships. Friendships blossomed like the corn and soybeans sprouting in the dark loam of that Midwest prairie. Leapfrogging cultural walls and social strata, people started liking each other. Rich and poor. Professor and student. Black and white. Blue-collar and white-collar. Farmer and physician. Jesus was the catalyst. Our love for Him drew us to each other.

It didn't matter who did what or who came from where or what side of town you lived on or what your major was. What mattered was that we loved Jesus and our hearts were knit together. Bonds forged in those days hold strong forty years later. We are friends for all time. Period.

Without question, the cornfields of Illinois are a universe removed from the snarled traffic of Washington, DC. But the friendship thing? Just the same. Titles play big in the most powerful city in the world. Prestige and rank reign in the hallowed halls. But when friendship arrives, all bets are off. It changes the game. It is the one thing that bridges the gap of status and power.

At a breakfast with some diplomats and former government officials, on the spur of the moment I was asked to offer a thought for the day. In my comments I lamented the truth that DC was not a town in which one wanted to toss his credentials on the table, because they would most certainly be trumped by someone. Someone who had more power, more money, more degrees, more years, more connections, more experience. More anything.

When I finished talking, one of the conveners, a former cabinet member to the president of the United States, said, "That's true, Dick, with one exception. If your credentials say 'Friend,' everyone wins."

"Friend" is the greatest title and the highest rank you can hold. No one knew this better than our soldiers in WWII. War is the antithesis of friendship. But friendship is the reason for staying in the fight. In WWII, army rangers from all kinds of backgrounds knew that. After being wounded, regular army soldiers were reassigned to different units. Airborne Rangers, on the other hand, were reunited with their same company after rehabilitation. The same guys they had fought with, eaten with, and laughed with from the beginning of their service became their bunkmates again.[1] The bond between them had been forged during arduous weeks of training in England long before they engaged the enemy. As Stephen Ambrose wrote, "Most of what they learned in the training proved to be valuable in combat, but it was that intimacy, that total trust, that comradeship that developed on those long, cold, wet English nights that proved to be invaluable."[2]

Bonding occurs in lots of ways. The first time I stepped into Giddings School with Mark and Lora and those nineteen people in Washington, DC, I was transported back to a house church in Urbana, Illinois, where Ruth and I first met with a bunch of university students. When Mark had to change locations because of zoning issues, I recalled moving to the board room of the YMCA on the university campus because our original location had been needed by an adjacent hospital. Although I was a westerner and Mark was a midwesterner, we found the geography of the kingdom brought us together. Once you've been in the trenches, you never forget!

When Jesus calls His disciples, they too are a disparate bunch. A handful of fishermen, a zealot, a tax collector, a swindler—all brought together by the Son of God in the flesh. They have some serious issues. But He apparently likes them. He sees their value. More than just followers, they are His friends. It is about mission and spirit and truth. Where Jesus goes, they go. What He does, they do. The reality that Jesus describes and embodies becomes the dream, the tracks on which they run. Jesus tells them:

> My command is this: Love each other as I have loved you. Greater love has no one than this: to lay down one's life for one's friends. You are my friends if you do what I command. I no longer call you servants, because a servant does not know his master's business. Instead, I have called you friends, for everything that I learned from my Father I have made known to you.[3]

Friendship is vulnerable and sacrificial. It permeates the deepest places of our souls. So William Butler Yeats speaks a deep truth when he says, "Think where man's glory most begins and ends, and say my glory was I had such friends."[4] You cannot negate the strength of friendship. You cannot underestimate the durability of a bond forged in the fires of adversity. You cannot belittle the force of prayers prayed on behalf of those we simply "like."

In friendship we get to look like Jesus, journeying two by two, arm in arm, becoming more than we could ever be by ourselves. We are designed for this grand company. And that is powerful stuff.

Mark's Story

My father-in-law, Bob Schmidgall, was one of the godliest men I've ever known. When I married his daughter, Lora, I also married into the Schmidgall family. My father-in-law became a mentor to me—someone I wanted to model my life after.

Bob Schmidgall loved his family deeply. I've never met anyone more passionate about missions. His compassion for people was contagious. His desire to hear God's voice resulted in lots of early mornings waiting on the Lord in prayer. And there was one more thing that I loved about Dad—his love of laughter, especially when he was drinking hot chocolate and it would come out of his nose because of an impromptu joke. He had a joy about life that was infectious. It impacted the way he lived and worked. And he liked to be around people he could laugh with too. He used to say, "Who you are doing ministry with will determine how much you enjoy it." He was right.

In my opinion, fulfillment in any occupation is 49 percent portfolio. You certainly want to find your sweet spot—the place where your God-given gifts and God-ordained passions overlap. But 51 percent of fulfillment has to do with the chemistry of the people you're working with. This I know for sure: I want to *do ministry* with people I want to *do life* with. That principle has shaped the way I lead our staff. We work hard. We play hard. And we laugh even harder.

One of the things that defines our culture at National Community Church is our theology of fun. We take God seriously, but we don't take ourselves seriously. We have cultivated a culture of honor, but we've also cultivated a culture of humor. Those two things aren't unrelated. The healthiest, holiest, and happiest people on the planet are those who laugh at themselves the most. And when you add someone else to the mix, it gets even better. Victor Borge said, "Laughter is the shortest distance between two people." Laughter forms an emotional, spiritual, and physiological bond that can't be quickly broken. Humor is hardwired into our church's DNA, and it comes from the top down. Everyone who really knows me knows that I have a goofy side, and I'm not ashamed of it. If chocolate cake is on the menu, some of it will undoubtedly end up on my front teeth. I love sneaking up on people and giving them a big ol' chocolate grin. It never gets old . . . to me! Makes *me* laugh every time. In fact, if I can convince my family to do it, I'd like chocolate on my teeth when I'm finally laid to rest. I want one last laugh!

Laughter is a litmus test when it comes to who we hire at National Community Church. The number one personality trait I look for is a sense of humor. If you can't laugh at my jokes, we can't work together. Life is too short and ministry is too hard not to have a little fun along the way! I don't think we've ever had a staff meeting or church gathering without a measure of laughter. And I never want to, because that would be boring. While I love the words *fun* and *loving* by themselves, the combination of both is even better: *fun-loving*. It's like the combination of Ruth and Chris into my favorite restaurant: Ruth's Chris Steak House. They belong together.

In my parlance, CEO stands for Chief Emotional Officer. You don't just set the pace as a leader. You set the tone. According to author and psychologist Daniel Goleman, emotional intelligence accounts for 80 percent of career success.[5] If that's true, then I'd better do my best to foster an atmosphere of emotional positivity. It starts with operating in a spirit of humility. Throw in the fruit of the Spirit—love, joy, peace, patience, kindness, goodness, gentleness, faithfulness, and self-control—and you've got the ingredients for a dream team.

Every summer our staff gets out of the city for our annual Play and Pray retreat. There is nothing on the agenda other than praying and playing. We play Settlers of Catan late into the night. We pull out the karaoke machine. We spend extended times praying into each other's lives. And it's not just staff. It's spouses and children too. It's like a family reunion, and the relational capital from that one retreat carries over into our meetings and our ministries the rest of the year.

Every team meeting at NCC starts by sharing wins. Call them *testimonies* if you want. Whatever you don't turn into praise turns into pride. So we want to be careful to give God all of the glory. After all, it's the one thing He won't share! Along with giving God the glory, we also celebrate each person's unique contribution to the team effort with our patented slow clap. I want to make sure every member of our team feels valued, not just for *what they do* but more importantly for *who they are*. One way we celebrate uniqueness is by giving every staff member at NCC the Myers-Briggs personality assessment as well as the StrengthsFinder assessment. It's one of the ways we applaud each other's uniqueness and play off of it.

Have you ever noticed Jesus' knack for nicknames? I've tried to follow suit. In fact, I have at least one nickname for just about everybody on staff. Our digital pastor, Matt Ortiz, is *Tera Matt*, as in terabyte. Our campus pastor in Berlin, Germany, John

Hasler, probably has the most nicknames. My personal favorite? *The German Shepherd*. Of course, Foth is just Foth. His name is his nickname. Sort of like Bono, Usher, or the artist formerly known as Prince, Foth is a mononym.

The nicknames that Jesus gave were not descriptive as much as they were prescriptive. Simon Peter was anything but a *Rock*. Impetuous is more like it. The *Sons of Thunder*, James and John? With her boys in tow, their mother asked Jesus if her sons could sit at his right and and left hand. More like mama's boys! But Jesus saw potential where others didn't. Those nicknames were more than terms of endearment. They were prophetic words that completely revolutionized who those people saw when they looked in the mirror. Jesus didn't just see what was wrong with people. He saw what was right.

By the time my school loans were paid off, my college education was almost completely forgotten. But one statement from one lecture will be a lifelong motto. The funny thing is that it wasn't even from one of my professors. It was a guest lecturer named Jeff Swaim who said, "Catch people doing things right." It's much easier catching people doing things wrong! That comes naturally. The opposite comes supernaturally. But it's far more fun!

Not long ago, Dave Ramsey invited a few dozen pastors to spend a few days with him in Nashville. I didn't know Dave well, but I quickly learned that he is someone who has turned this idea into an art form. For starters, he rented out the Country Music Hall of Fame and put on a private concert by some of country music's finest songwriters. He threw in a few gifts, including a saddlebag by Colonel Littleton.[6] But there's one statement that I think encapsulates who Dave is and what he's about. He said, "Sometimes you have to give the waitress at Waffle House a $100 tip just to see another human being do the Snoopy dance!" So true. So fun.

One of my favorite pastimes is overtipping or tipping people who don't typically get tipped. If you want to make a server's day by making a statement, give them a tip that is larger than the bill. Or tip someone when they least expect it. I have profound respect for anyone who does a job I wouldn't particularly want to do, like cleaning an airport bathroom. Occasionally, I'll give someone like that a tip. I make sure that it's legal, and I never want it to come across as condescending in any way. A tip is just a genuine token of appreciation. It's also one way of catching people doing things right. And it can turn an ordinary moment into a little adventure.

Catch People Doing Things Right

6

Stepping Stones

Riding in a wagon for two hundred miles is not for sissies.

In 1905 the United States was a place that brimmed with possibilities. In an effort begun by President Benjamin Harrison in 1889 to settle the unassigned territories, President Teddy Roosevelt was handing out 160-acre parcels of Oklahoma farmland on a first-come, first-served basis. Whoever got there first won the prize. In the original allocation, some even started a bit early to beat the rush. To this day they are known as "Sooners."

A couple hundred miles north of the Oklahoma line, in the small town of Hillsboro, Kansas, a family took Roosevelt up on his offer. They loaded a wagon with food, feed, and supplies for the long journey. Jerry and Sara were leaving behind everything they knew—family, friends, and comforts of home. The journey was uncertain and the destination unfamiliar. They were risking all they had in the hope of something better. Hearts thumping, they clambered up into the wagon, tucked their four children in behind them, and with the clatter of horse hooves and the creak of wagon wheels, headed into their future.

In late July 1993, Ruth and I found ourselves in a place like that. There we sat once again in Modesto, California, in front of her parents' home. Just like November of 1966, when we headed for Illinois.

The smell of ripe peaches was in the air as the summer heat baked the orchards around the house. The twenty-six-foot U-Haul truck was loaded and the leftovers stored in the tractor shed. We were heading to Washington, DC. An invitation to the capital had been extended with this question: "Why don't you bring your gifts and your group of friends and mix them with our gifts and our group of friends, and together let's be light in a dark place?"

This would be no Moses role. Instead of running a college, I would be meeting one-on-one in private settings. There were several noes in the equation: no salary, no office, no staff, and no title. We were leaving two of our three college-age children behind, along with our eldest daughter and her husband who had just had our first grandchild. We were selling our home and moving into a rental. It felt a little crazy. It was a little crazy. Quite a few of our friends thought we were crazy.

Going from the known to the unknown is always daunting. Leaving friends and family behind stretched us to the limit. More than that, moving across country at fifty-one years of age was way more challenging than doing it at twenty-three. But that's what risk is. With only a sketch of what the future might hold, Ruth and I were looking a lot like my great-grandparents, Jerry and Sara Foth. We were loading up the wagon and heading out. It turned out to be some of the most rewarding years of our lives.

"Easy risk" is an oxymoron. Risks don't come easy. They leave us exposed. Our personal identity goes up for grabs. A year into our time in Washington, I was still working inside my brain to find my place. What was a blue-collar kid from the streets of Oakland doing trying to reach out to Washington's elite? I'm not a blueblood. I did not attend an Ivy League school. And I'm a West Coaster, not an East Coaster.

Walking through the Russell Senate Office Building one morning to meet with a senator, I felt anxious. In that moment I heard Jesus say, "Foth, if you speak with the King of the universe in the morning, it is not so difficult to speak to a United States senator in the afternoon." A little perspective never hurts.

Risk taking really has to do with surrender. Letting go of comfort for discomfort. Releasing control. Stepping out of the boat. Jumping off the cliff. It's simply not natural. It is being talked into doing a canopy tour, like I did a few years back, with a harness connected to a steel zip line ten thousand feet up in the Ecuadorian Andes with my friend Barry Noonan and our two sons, Chris and Kirk. Leaping off a platform, you soar over the valley floor five hundred feet below. And you pick up speed as you go—uncomfortable speed because mass times velocity equals momentum. Then there's the rain and the thick leather gloves designed to create friction on the steel cable to slow you down that become, in a word, useless. Let's just say I'm grateful to be alive.

I learned something to do with surrender that day. Surrender has a terrifying exhilaration to it. It is trusting someone and something other than yourself. It is totally counterintuitive.

My friend Rich Dixon is by training a middle school math teacher. He likes things that are measurable. In the fall of 2012, he and his wife, Becky, and their dog, Monty, started on a measurable journey with immeasurable outcomes and a high-risk adventure. They took a bike ride, but not just any bike ride.

Almost thirty years ago Rich fell off his roof while putting up Christmas lights and ended up in a wheelchair. After ten years of depression, someone introduced him to hand cycling. In September of 2012, he and Becky decided to ride into the face of what some might call hopeless circumstances with a message of hope. They embarked on a hand-cycling journey from the headwaters of the Mississippi in Lake Itasca, Minnesota, to New Orleans, Louisiana—a trek of 1,600 miles.

Two things happened: they raised over $60,000 for Convoy of Hope, a group that helps the poor and disenfranchised around the world, and they had countless and sometimes miraculous encounters with people along the way.[1] Simply put, it was high risk, high impact, high reward.

Mark is a guy who risks by pushing boundaries. The unknown for him is a siren song. He should probably have "high risk, high reward" tattooed on his right bicep. He's a person who when the barista says, "Cream or sugar with your coffee?" should probably say "No thanks. Just adrenaline!" Renting a theater at Union Station in DC when you don't know where the money is coming from. Building a coffeehouse on Capitol Hill as material prices skyrocket around the world. And planting another coffeehouse in Berlin, Germany, while doing new sites in the DC metro area. All those moves make the point.

In kingdom work, things have a way of coming back around! We serve a God who values hearts over titles and loves turning our perceptions inside out. Risk is the currency of good adventure. "Take up your cross, and follow me"[2] is not an invitation for the faint of heart. You can count on feeling vulnerable and insecure. You can count on being out of your depth and in over your head. But the call to adventure is Spirit calling to spirit. Deep calling to deep. It is what you are made for. And if you can truly surrender to Him, you will do more, be more, experience more. Life will just be more.

Surrendering to Jesus of Nazareth is a paradox. It is absolute risk and it is no risk at all. When it comes to my fear of being disappointed one more time, I'm encouraged by Paul's words:

> For it is with your heart that you believe and are justified, and it is with your mouth that you profess your faith and are saved.

As Scripture says, "Anyone who believes in him will never be put to shame."[3]

Jim Elliot, a missionary to the Huaorani tribe, said it this way: "He is no fool who gives what he cannot keep to gain that which he cannot lose."[4] You don't lose your life when you choose to follow Jesus—it is the starting point to the life you were meant to live. Why not risk it all and throw in your lot with the King of the universe?

It's time to load up the wagon and head into your future!

Mark's Story

It's amazing how much you know when you're twenty-two.

That's when I put together a twenty-five-year strategic plan to plant a church on the north shore of Chicago. My professor gave it an A. In reality, it got an F. Our first attempt at church planting was a fail, but it laid the foundation for everything God has done at National Community Church in Washington, DC. I learned an invaluable lesson: "unless the LORD builds the house, those who build it labor in vain"![5] It was also the catalyst that gave us the courage to load up our wagon, a fifteen-foot U-Haul, and take a 595-mile step of faith. Like the Foths, we had our fair share of *noes*: no salary and no place to live. But we also knew that every adventure begins with saying *yes* to God's will, God's way. Then it's *game on*.

Some people consider risk a four-letter word. Any opportunity that could lead to the possibility of failure is something to be avoided at all costs. They want the safety of success without the risk of failure. Fear of failure keeps them hemmed in, making the same small choices. Low risk. Low reward. I have a different way of looking at life. I fear missing out on opportunity more than making mistakes. I certainly count costs, but not just the actual costs. I take a long hard look at opportunity costs. As I see it, you can either avoid making mistakes and play not to lose, or you can make the most of every opportunity and play to win. I live by a simple premise: the greatest risk is taking no risks at all. If you don't get out of the boat, one thing is sure, you will never walk on water.

Some of the greatest innovators and leaders of our time had repeated failures. Not just one or two failures but life-defining moments that could have and should have stopped them in their tracks. Abraham Lincoln lost eight elections and had two failed business ventures and a nervous breakdown before he ever set foot in the Oval Office. It took Thomas Edison over ten thousand tries to get the lightbulb right. Most of us would have given up after two or three attempts. After years of trying to harness electricity as a light source, he was asked by a reporter if he felt like a failure. He looked surprised and said, "Young man, why would I feel like a failure? And why would I ever give up? I now know definitively over nine thousand ways that an electric lightbulb will not work. Success is almost in my grasp."[6]

The leading cause of failure is mismanaged success. And the leading cause of success is well-managed failure. A thousand tries later, a small flicker danced on the first working lightbulb filament and revolutionized the entire world. Nothing would ever be the same again. Edison could have given up years earlier and saved face. He could have come up with some small invention he knew would work to restore his reputation. He could have quit risking and played it safe, but he looked at life through a different lens than his doubters. He didn't see his failures as failures. He saw them as necessary stepping stones that were leading him closer and closer to where he needed to be.

I have had more than my share of epic fails. Ever heard of the Godipod? Probably not. That is because it was one of my good ideas that turned out to be a bad idea! I thought it was a million-dollar idea, but it turned out to be a $15,000 net loss. Actually, it was a $15,000 education. Our first church plant was embarrassing, discouraging, and confusing. So when we were asked to pastor a congregation of nineteen on Capitol Hill two years later, we could have said, "No, thanks. Been there. Done that." But even though our first attempt had failed, we felt this was an opportunity we couldn't pass up.

As Edison is credited with saying, "Opportunity is missed by most people because it is dressed in overalls and looks like work."[7] We all want to be successful, but most of us aren't willing to do what those who are successful did to attain it. We want success without sacrifice, but you can't have one without the other!

Abraham Lincoln, on the heels of repeated political failure, offered this challenge: "My great concern is not whether you have failed, but whether you are content with your failure."[8] Falling down is *not* failure. The only way you can fail is if you stay down. Success is getting back up time and time again.

We tend to overestimate what we can accomplish in a year or two, but we underestimate what God can accomplish in a decade or two. The key? Keep doing the right thing day in and day out, week in and week out, year in and year out. Temporary setbacks are just that—temporary. Zoom out. Look at the big picture. If your dream is from God, it'll probably take longer and be harder than anything you imagine. But that simply means it's a God-sized goal. I want to go after dreams that are destined to fail without divine intervention.

A long obedience in the same direction.[9]

That's where it's at, as far as I'm concerned. It's the key to longevity. It's the key to legacy. I'm less and less impressed with people who experience short order success. I'm more and more impressed with people who simply keep on keeping on. I love the phrase "little by little" in Exodus 23:30. We want a lot by a lot, but that's not the way it works in God's kingdom ventures. Malcolm Gladwell refers to it as the "ten-thousand-hour rule."[10] If you really want to get good at anything, you've got to work at it for ten thousand hours. You can't cheat the system. And I see that in Dick Foth.

After some of his best sermons, I'll jokingly tell him, "If you keep at this preaching thing, you could get pretty good someday." Hey, someone has to keep him humble! The reality is this: Foth's messages are not the by-product of forty hours of study. More like ten thousand hours of living. That's where the gravitas comes from. And as good as his sermons are, his life is even better.

Does the thought of making a big mistake keep you sidelined? Or does the fear of losing out on your next opportunity motivate you to risk it all? Does your latest failed experiment have you shaking your head in discouragement? Or does it motivate you toward your next big win? Are you content with failing, or do you see it as a catapult to your next adventure? Some suggest that a successful life is a single upward trajectory of one win laid on top of the next. God says, "I will take your biggest failures and use them to my advantage." Your ability to see failure as a necessary stepping stone directly correlates with your ability to dream bigger and dream better. If you are willing to risk it all and step out in faith, God can recycle your mistakes. I have some more good failures in front of me. And in return, I believe they will yield more opportunities, more leaps of faith, more wins, and more successes. Safety is highly overrated. Why not risk it all and live the life you were meant to live?

The Greatest Risk Is
Taking No Risks at All

7

Shared Goals

 Dick's Story

Airplanes are funny things. In a mere fifty years they have supplanted trains and ships as the primary form of rapid transit around the world. They are unnatural. Not just because you speed at five hundred miles per hour six miles above the surface of the earth. They are unnatural because you can sit elbow to elbow with a total stranger for five hours as you cross America, and upon deplaning you are still strangers.

My favorite way of getting around that is a question. I turn to my seatmate and say, "So, are you going home or leaving home?" Many interesting conversations ensue.

One such chat, some years ago, was special. I was on a flight from Chicago to a southern city seated next to a young guy with dark glasses and thick, wavy hair. He was a corporate salesman heading home from a conference. I thought conversation might not be high on his list, because he kept his sunglasses on. But as we winged our way south, the small talk changed to real talk. The kind of talk that reveals your soul.

At one point I asked him, "What are your three goals in life?"

He thought a moment and then said, "Why don't you tell me your three first, and I'll tell you mine?"

On the spur of the moment I said, "Number one, I always want to find myself in the kingdom of God; number two, I always want to have tight relationships with people; number three, I never want to stop adventuring all of my life."

He said, "Well, I think those would be my three too! But would it be okay if I made a hundred grand this year?" In 1971, $100,000 was huge money.

"Sure!" I told him. If we're going to have goals, let's shoot for the moon!

"By 'kingdom,'" he said, continuing the conversation, "do you mean Jesus?"

"Yes."

"I used to think about Jesus. When I was twelve I actually began following Jesus at a summer camp. But I wandered off in high school, and I've never gotten back."

He paused for a moment. I couldn't read his expression through his dark glasses.

"I've got to tell you, when I go on trips like this, the first thing I do is get a bottle and go to a motel room, and it's downhill from there."

Advice didn't seem appropriate. Just an invitation. "It would be great," I said, "if you would come back."

When we landed, he stepped into the aisle to let me out because he was going on. When I faced him, he took off his sunglasses and stuck his hand out. Then I surprised myself by saying, "I think God sent me to you."

"I think so too," he agreed. Sometimes divine appointments happen in Row 7 of a DC-9.

My parting suggestion was, "Why don't you find somebody in your town who is a believer and just start coming back? I'll follow up with you in a couple weeks and see how you are doing."

When I called him three weeks later, he said, "I've found somebody to meet with, and I'm coming back."

Goals have a way of refocusing your life. They give you purpose and a target to shoot for. They are the compass of our dreams, helping us set a steady course. Goals comprise direction and progress. When we lose sight of our goals, we tend to lose sight of ourselves and who we are trying to become, who God has made us to be.

My friend was most definitely pursuing his goal of making $100,000 a year. But what came into focus in our conversation was that he had lost sight of himself. The boy who loved Jesus. The man who respected himself. These were lost in translation.

I'm reminded of a trip I took with some great friends a decade ago. We were a dozen men from different walks of life—educators, clergymen, politicians, lawyers, and a long-net fisherman from North Carolina, all connected to my boyhood friend, Senator John Ashcroft. We would meet once a year for a long weekend just to enjoy life and each other. It was a time to recalibrate. This particular weekend would be spent on Catalina Island, off the coast of southern California.

The Four Preps, a popular American quartet in the fifties, sixties, and seventies, sang of Catalina this way: "Twenty-six miles across the sea, Santa Catalina is a-waitin' for me!" On a late fall afternoon we traversed those twenty-six miles in three eighteen-foot open fishing boats. When I inquired of my lawyer friend, who was coordinating the small flotilla, about the clouds out over the Catalina Channel, he replied, "Oh, we just call that a marine layer." Not much later, as night fell and we were five miles out in the channel, that marine layer exploded in thunder and lightning.

Water poured over the sides of the boat as it pitched in the dark seas. The lightning strikes were nonstop. Tired, wet, and not a little disconcerted, we desperately tried to see Catalina. About that time lightning struck so close that it knocked out our loran, the radar device that showed our position in relationship to land. Now, except for those flashes, we were blind. The problem? If we missed Catalina, our next stop was Hawaii—2,459 miles away! Gratefully, we soon saw winking lights on the beach showing us the harbor.

Life is full of goals to be identified and kept in sight. When we lose sight of the goal, we simply drift. Sometimes drift can mean disaster.

My friend Paul McGarvey had a phrase he posted in the locker room for his football team. It read, "Without desire— disaster!" Among the towels and helmets and gear, there was a call to something greater. At the gut level this team had to actually *want* to win before it could happen. All the practices, all the drills, all the sweat, and all the hustle had to be fueled by that desire. If they didn't have the desire, the game was lost before they stepped foot on the field.

The same is true for this adventure we call life. We have to have the desire to reach our goals. Desire moves mountains and breaks down walls. Sometimes we get off course, desiring things or setting goals that will lead to no good end. But if our desire is in the right place, loving Jesus and loving others, there is no telling where Jesus can take us. He out-dreams us, out-plans us, and outdoes us every time.

Philippians 2:13 says, "For it is God who works in you, both to will and to work for his good pleasure" (ESV).

We may not meet every goal that we set. We may or may not see that $100,000 we were hoping for. We will make some mistakes and do a little backtracking now and again. But one thing is clear: if our greatest desire is to follow Jesus and our greatest goal is to find ourselves in His presence at the end of this life, He will make it so. In that moment, our desire and His desire for us will intersect.

Mark's Story

In 1905 Albert Einstein stunned the world with his revolutionary equation, $E = mc^2$. Einstein wrote hundreds of papers over the course of his career. But this provocative equation, printed in one of his *Annus Mirabilis* papers, wasn't something he just stumbled upon by chance. It was the culmination of years of research, an insatiable curiosity about the universe, and a deep love of science. When Einstein was a small boy, his father gave him a compass. Albert was mesmerized by the power that seemed to emanate from within the magnetic pull of the compass. He would write years later, "I can still remember . . . that this experience made a deep and lasting impression on me. Something deeply hidden had to be behind things."[1] As a teenager, the intrigue and wonder of physics crept into Albert's dreams. One night, he dreamed he was sledding down a hill, faster and faster, until he approached the speed of light. The stars radiated a broad spectrum of colors. He was entranced. When he awoke, he knew he had to understand the dream. In later years he said that his entire scientific career was a meditation on that dream.

Albert Einstein didn't understand the dream he had when he was thirteen, but something deep inside him kept pondering this dream his entire life. He may not have set tangible goals for himself to shoot for, but each failed experiment, each new discovery was one step closer to understanding the speed of light. Each science class and professorship he took was moving him closer toward his destiny.

When I was a seminary student, my dreams were a little different. I had to go in for an interview to be officially credentialed as a minister. I expected theological questions, and I was prepared for those. But the wise old pastor sitting across from me didn't ask me theological questions about Scripture. He asked me about me: "If you had to describe yourself in one word, what would it be?"

That was not the question I was anticipating. But without hesitation I said, "Driven."

I actually thought it was a good answer at the time. I thought they might even bypass the licensing process and just ordain me on the spot. "Hey guys, we've got a driven twenty-two-year-old on our hands!" I had a lot of dreams I wanted to accomplish, and I wanted to do it as quickly as possible. I still do. But over the years, I have shifted from an ASAP to an ALAT approach to life. It's not about accomplishing my goals *as soon as possible*. It's about *as long as it takes*.

If I had to describe myself in one word now? *Seeker.* At twenty-two, I was driven by the desire to accomplish things for God. Twenty-two years later, it's not about seeking success. It's about seeking God. And when you seek God, success will follow. March 23, 2014, is one of my defining days. That's the day I made a covenant to seek the Lord. I had been serving God for nearly two decades at that juncture, but I wasn't seeking Him like I could have or should have. At least not *first*.[2] And God will never settle for second place. So I'm going after God with a new intensity, a new consistency. But that doesn't mean I'm dreaming any less. The more time you spend in the presence of God, the bigger your dreams become.

I came up with my first life goal list in my twenties. Over the course of a decade, I have continued to add more goals while checking off a few. Every year, I prioritize which ones I should go after that year. For me, it's a stewardship issue. I am trying to steward whatever gifts God has given to me by putting them in goal form.

I am called to write. That has segued into a goal of writing twenty-five books. One of our family values is generosity. The amount that we target to give away each year is an expression of our belief that, in the words of Jesus, "it is more blessed to give than to receive."[3] My travel and experience goals have a theological foundation in the belief that if God created everything, it is good stewardship to study and explore and enjoy all the different facets of His creation. Each goal I have set is directly linked to a unique facet of how God has wired me and the dreams He has placed within me.

A few years ago, the tectonic plates shifted in my goal-setting. My first goal list was quite self-centered. In recent years I have adapted my goals by making them more relational. For example, I wouldn't really want to see a Broadway play all by myself, but seeing a Broadway play with Summer is a wonderful memory. Taking her to see *Mary Poppins* doubled the joy because I experienced it with her. Kissing Lora on top of the Eiffel Tower was far more fun than seeing it for myself. And I wouldn't have even gone to Super Bowl XLV if I couldn't have taken Josiah with me.

By nature, I'm task oriented. By nurture, and with a little mentoring from Foth, I'm becoming more relationship oriented. I'll never be as relational as Dick—to be honest, I'm not real talkative on flights! But I want to invest in others the way Dick has invested in me. I'm not just interested in what people can bring to our team; I am thinking about how I can help fan into flame the gifts God has given them. I think of church as a two-lane highway. One lane is inviting people to be part of the corporate dream God has given National Community Church. But I love the second lane even more: being part of the individual dream God has given them.

For several years, NCC member Jill Carmichael served as the division director at Friendship Place, an agency that offers supportive housing for the most vulnerable and chronically homeless in DC. Jill's passion for the homeless is contagious. It inspired twenty-four others from NCC to take the homeless challenge this year and spend seventy-two hours on the streets of DC. Their goal is to end homelessness in the nation's capital. Now that is a vision we can get behind.

Goals are a way to go after things and live life to the fullest. When you are going after a goal together, with people you care about, it cements a relationship unlike anything else. If we share all that God has put in our hearts and are stewarding our gifts and talents collectively in His name, the sky is the limit!

There is only one Albert Einstein. There is only one Jill Carmichael. There is only one Dick Foth. There is only one you. No two passions, no two goals, no two people will ever be exactly the same. When God created us He didn't make us variations on a theme; He created a complete original. He designed us with different passions, different purposes, and different desires. God has crafted specific dreams for us and crafted us specifically for those dreams.

The last time I checked, faith is being sure of what we hope for.[4] That sounds an awful lot like goals. God-glorifying goals. So becoming goal oriented is really the by-product of becoming God oriented. You can't help but dream about the future. And it's those God-sized dreams that keep us on our knees in raw dependence upon God. That's what keeps us humble, keeps us hungry. That's what keeps us pressing in and pressing on.

Goals Are Dreams with Deadlines

8

The Locus of Love

Surfers know the name Steamer Lane. It is a spot that hosts the annual Coldwater Classic surfing competition and dead-ends into West Cliff Drive in Santa Cruz, California. The street mirrors the natural curve of the Pacific coastline, winding from the turn-of-the-century boardwalk amusement park, up past Steamer Lane at Lighthouse Point and Seal Rock, hugging the salt-sprayed cliffs until it ends at the long sweep of Natural Bridges State Beach. It was my favorite place to run when I was a college president.

Walking along its adjoining bike path, you take in a symphony of sights, sounds, and smells. The call of the gulls, the bite of salt in the wind, and the swell of the waves crashing against jutting rock form a breathtaking multisensory experience.

On a cool night in the spring of 1962, many years before those runs, I was experiencing a different sensation as I drove along West Cliff Drive. It was the thudding of my heart in my chest. Sitting in the seat next to me was Ruth Blakeley, a tall, green-eyed girl who, as the dean of women of our college said, "carried herself like a queen." We had been going out for about six months, but I was still nervous about our relationship. A twenty-year-old college junior, I had been stuttering since the age of five. Feeling a bit insecure about this, I mentioned it offhandedly to Ruth.

"Ruth, I d-d-don't know if you w-w-would w-w-want to keep g-going with m-me because I st-st . . . can't talk."

She looked at me, smiled very sweetly, and said, "Oh, really? I hadn't noticed."

That affirmation started something. It started unlocking a door and letting me out. She freed up my soul. Because what I heard her say was, *I like you the way you are. I like you whether you stutter or not.*

When you are a stutterer, it doesn't feel like a physical impairment, it feels like a personality disorder. Growing up, I felt like half the time people were looking me in the mouth and they thought I was stupid. Stuttering made me feel like I was less than. So when Ruth smiled at me and said she hadn't noticed my stuttering, my world shifted on its axis. She loved me as I was. In her eyes, I was all I needed to be. She framed one of the keys to my life. She was loving me the way I needed to be loved.

Years ago my friend Alan Groff shared this definition: "love is the accurate estimate and the adequate supply of another person's need." That truth has stuck with me. In the English language, *love* is an accordion word—it can contract or expand depending on the focus. "I love baseball. I love peanut butter. I love you." The word ends up devoid of meaning. It doesn't *say* anything. But if *love* really means that we accurately estimate and adequately supply another person's need, it says a ton. It becomes unique and powerful and life-giving.

Usually, when we say we love someone, we don't accurately estimate anything. We just love people the way *we* want to be loved. We think if we want to be loved a certain way, everyone else should too.

In his later years, my dad, who lived in Palm Springs, California, showed us his love each Christmas by sending us dates. Jellied dates, powdered dates, dates stuffed with walnuts. He really loved dates. Unfortunately we didn't. We ended up with seventy-eight pounds of dates in our refrigerator over the years, but I could never work up the nerve to tell him we didn't like them!

In addition to dates, Dad had a great fondness for cheese. One Christmas we sent Dad a ten-pound party pack of Wisconsin cheese. When he called to thank us for the cheese, he asked me, "Have I ever sent you dates for Christmas?" It was now or never.

I said, "Yes, quite a few times. And Dad, I've got to be honest. We are not so big on dates."

He said, "Oh, I'm sorry. I'll send you something else." Within a week we got a ten-pound box of cheese! At least it wasn't dates.

Loving people the way they need to be loved is never easy. It took me some years into our marriage to figure out how to love Ruth. When we were young parents with four kids ages eight and under, I would come home from work and find Ruth frazzled and smelling slightly like diaper rash cream.

With a wild look in her eye, she would say, "I've got to get out of here!" I thought I knew how to remedy that. I would get her out of the house and away from the kids. One Friday afternoon in late November, I came home and said, "Ruth, you are not going to believe this! I got two tickets to see the Fighting Illini play Ohio State!" She looked at me unsmiling and said, "Terrific."

Back then I thought I could love Ruth the way I wanted to be loved and it would all work out. But for Ruth, watching the Fighting Illini was a lot like getting a box of dates from my dad.

The last thing she wanted to do was spend three hours sitting in a snowy stadium watching guys knock each other down.

I'm a lot smarter now. I know that loving Ruth looks a whole lot more like a hot cup of tea, a bar of Hershey's chocolate, and a trip to an antique store. If we are going to live this life to the full, we have to begin loving each other the way we need to be loved. It may not come naturally, but if we do, it will revolutionize our friendships, our relationships with our spouses, and our interactions with our kids.

Loving people the way they need to be loved is the whole point of Jesus. Take a closer look at John 3:16: "For God so loved the world that he gave his one and only Son, that whoever believes in him shall not perish but have eternal life." Jesus understood what love looked like more than anyone else. He met us at the point of our greatest need. Let me paraphrase the verse this way: "For God so loved Richard Foth that He accurately estimated that he was a creep who needed a Redeemer. Therefore, He adequately supplied a Redeemer in the person of Jesus Christ of Nazareth so that Foth could live with Him forever. Therefore, Foth knows he is loved." That is the heart of it. Or as Mark puts it, "Jesus loves us when we least expect it and least deserve it!"

When we figure out *how* to love the other person, it unlocks our doors, frees up our souls, and sets us on the path to living the kind of life we are built for.

Mark's Story

Love is a powerful thing, and I have had the privilege of being loved in a powerful way. I have two of the most loving parents a person could ever want. They had that irrational parental type of faith in me that I could be whatever I wanted to be and do whatever I wanted to do. They believed in me, letting me believe in myself. I always knew that my mom and dad were in my corner. No matter what. But the amazing thing about my mom and dad is that they loved me even when I messed up. Those are the most memorable moments, like the day I dropped my grandfather's fossil. It happened again when I was a high school senior.

One afternoon when I was on the way to one of my basketball games, I took a sharp left turn and cut off a car that was coming in the opposite direction. Unfortunately, that car was one of those cars with lights and sirens on top of it! I actually tried to take a few side roads and ditch the police car because I knew the officer would be coming after me. Apparently, I was not that great at making a clean getaway. That's how I got my first ticket, with a $100 price tag—a small fortune to a high school kid making minimum wage in a part-time job at a gas station. I thought long and hard about what I should do. I decided that I wasn't going to tell my parents about it because, you know, I didn't want them to worry unnecessarily. I was a caring son! What I didn't know was that the Naperville police department had a practice of mailing a copy of the ticket to an offender's home address. Given the fact that my mom got the mail every day, she and my dad soon found out that I had been cited. So they knew, but I didn't know that they knew. I lived with my secret for quite some time. It ate away at me since I had no idea how I was going to pay the ticket.

The moment of truth came on the night of a basketball game against our crosstown rivals. We made an incredible comeback that night, erasing a 23-point deficit with five minutes left in the game. So it was an adrenaline high. Afterward my dad came down on the court. He didn't mention the win or the great game I had played. He just said, "Mark, I want you to know that we are going to pay that ticket for you." No recriminations. No "I'm so disappointed in you." Just "We've got this."

I have never felt two stronger emotions at the same time. I was filled with a deep sense of guilt upon discovering that my parents knew what I had done and an incredible sense of relief of knowing that they were taking care of the fine that I had no way of paying. It was a defining moment—a moment that defined grace. That singular moment in time has shaped the way I live my life today and the way I try to parent our kids. As a parent, you've got to know when to execute justice and discipline your children. You also need to know when to show mercy and model the grace of God. I look for opportunities to show my kids grace so that they can experience what it feels like. That sense of being loved, no matter what, sets you free.

This experience of grace has impacted the way we model grace at NCC too. Another one of our core values as a church is, *love people when they least expect it and least deserve it.* That is the kind of love Jesus shows to us. When we are at our worst, He is at His best. One of the best examples of that is shown in the story of a woman caught in the act of adultery. Here was a woman who knew she was wrong. In the presence of Jesus, she didn't expect grace, she expected to die. According to Mosaic law, she deserved to be stoned to death. But Jesus thought she deserved something different. The only One who had a right to pick up a stone and throw it was the One who came to her defense and loved her when she least expected it and least deserved it. The Pharisees were holding stones, and Jesus said, "Let any one of you who is without sin be the first to throw a stone at her."[1] It is almost like Jesus was saying, "You can stone her over my dead body!" He changed her death sentence into a new lease on life. Not only did she not have to die, but He offered her a new way to live. Where the Pharisees and the law had her cornered and trapped, Jesus stepped in with His love and set her free.

Over the years I have consistently quoted Dick's definition of love: *the accurate estimate and adequate supply of another*

87

person's need. That's what you do when you can't say it any better than it's already been said. So I quote Dick often, but the first time Dick quoted me, it almost felt like an out-of-body experience. If I'm not mistaken, it was this core value: *love people when they least expect it and least deserve it.* It was a strange role reversal, but that is one of the great joys of mentoring. Every once in a while, the student plays teacher. Call it reverse mentoring if you want. It turns mentoring into a two-way street.

The ability to love someone because they do what you want them to do is common. The ability to love someone despite what they have done, simply because of who they are, is rare. Yet Jesus shows us over and over in the Gospels that He loved people not because of what they did or didn't do. That wasn't the locus of love. He kept reaching out to the people who didn't expect to be loved—the outcasts, the misfits, the sinners. He didn't love them because of who they were. He loved them because of who He was.

There is something profound about a love that is not performance based. True love doesn't give grades. If it did, we'd all fail. But on the cross, we got a pass. Jesus took the test for us. He paid the $100 ticket. He loved us when we least expected it and least deserved it. And that's what sets us free.

Love People When They Least Expect It and Least Deserve It

9

Invaluable and Irreplaceable

August 24, AD 79, was like any other day on Italy's idyllic southern coast. Until 1:00 p.m. That's when Mount Vesuvius exploded. When the eruption subsided two days later, the nearby cities of Pompeii and Herculaneum lay under thirteen to twenty feet of hot ash. Thousands of people with no place to run had been killed by thermal shock.

Nineteen centuries later, Ruth and I saw the uncovered remains of those cities and tried to imagine it all. The raw fear. The chaos. The futility. We were tourists in a grotesque, mesmerizing graveyard. And the event that brought us there was the absolute opposite of what we were observing. We were looking at a place of death while attending a conference immediately across the Tyrrhenian Sea from Vesuvius. It was called "The Adventure of Living."

Being surprised by good is way better than being surprised by bad. Our best surprises have the touch of God on them and make an indelible imprint on our souls. "The Adventure of Living" in Sorrento, Italy, was one of those surprises. Some dear friends from Urbana, Illinois, sent us there. The trip coincided with my thirtieth birthday. On my best day I never could have imagined being given such a gift. The thought of driving down the Amalfi Coast with Lyman Coleman, who was a guru of the small group movement in the seventies, and his wife, Margaret, would never have entered my mind. Having lunch in an Italian fishing village with a legendary German theologian was something I couldn't have dreamed up on my own either. To be fair, I wasn't astute enough really to know who these men were.

But sometimes our best moments come when God surprises us with things we haven't earned and certainly don't deserve. It shapes the way we see the world for the rest of our lives. That conference not only was the best birthday present I ever received but shifted the trajectory of my life.

The view across a cobalt sea from the open French doors of our room in the Grand Hotel Riviera was stunning. Below us a wooden pier lined with blue-and-white striped sun chairs jutted into the crystal water. Mount Vesuvius was sketched against the distant sky. Opening the windows, we inhaled the fragrance of orange trees in blossom.

The company was just as stimulating. Faculty consisted of writers, theologians, psychiatrists, and musicians, each one bringing a flavor and specialty to the mix. A hundred and twenty folks, most middle-aged and well-to-do. And then there was Ruth and me, who were neither. It is possible to be curious and a curiosity at one and the same time. That was us.

We were dropped into this fertile environment and encouraged to make contact and have meals with the speakers. We were on cloud nine. We had a lunch with counselor Paul Tournier and psychiatrist Bernard Harnik. We became friends with Lyman and Margaret Coleman. Each conversation was brimming with new insights and laughter. Each new thought challenged us and left us excited to be a part of following God in this adventure of living. The week was spent soaking up the wisdom of some of the most forward-thinking leaders of the day. But we were most surprised by spontaneous encounters and conversations with our main speaker, Dr. Helmut Thielicke of Göttingen University in West Germany.

Helmut Thielicke was a German Lutheran theologian who had been part of the Goerdeler group along with well-known pastor Dietrich Bonhoeffer during World War II. Carl Goerdeler, a rising politician, gathered a network of military and political allies working toward the overthrow of the Nazi government and the downfall of Hitler. Helmut was a young theologian at the time and a leader in what would be called the Confessing Church. It stood against Hitler and the Nazi regime, which had hijacked the national church, using its pulpits as a means to spout Nazi rhetoric and dogma. Helmut escaped the Gestapo, unlike many of his counterparts, because he was young and wasn't as well known. An esteemed theologian and highly educated academic, Helmut's talks were riveting and thought provoking. Around the dinner table, we found him to be funny, down-to-earth, and a masterful storyteller.

We had the great privilege of spending an unplanned afternoon with Helmut and his wife, Marie-Luise, and their interpreter in the charming village of Positano, where he regaled us with stories of the war. Our final time with him took place at the closing dinner of the conference at the Grand Hotel Palatino in Rome. Nestled in a small ballroom, surrounded by the muted sounds of conversation and a bounty of food, we had the good fortune to be seated at his table. When our meal came to a close, Marie-Luise reached inside her purse and pulled out an old leather pouch from which she drew a fat, black cigar. She cut off the tip and gave it to him, and he began once again to share some of his stories with us. The man had lived an amazing life and then some.

I had asked him earlier if I could interview him for my Saturday morning radio program, *Wake Up and Live*, carried on the local CBS affiliate in Champaign-Urbana, Illinois. So we stepped away from the ballroom to record the interview through his interpreter, and I asked him to share about his involvement in the German resistance and about his faith. As the interview ended, I asked him one last question: "If you had one thing to say about God and man, what would you say?"

He paused, switched to English, and said, "Man is not valuable because he loves God. Man is valuable because God loves him."

Talk about a thundering one-liner. I knew that, but I didn't *know* that. Helmut Thielicke, this battle-tested warrior with a brilliant mind and a thousand anecdotes, had framed a principle that challenged my need to be loved because I performed well.

The way he did it, in a simple couplet, would come to mind twenty-five years later when I listened to Mark start framing his insights and ideas. He's a one-sentence master. When he says things like, "Prayer is the difference between the best you can do and the best God can do," it's a Thielicke moment for me.

Sometimes God speaks through His Word. Sometimes He speaks in a still small voice. Sometimes He speaks through a young pastor-entrepreneur in Washington, DC. And sometimes God speaks to you through a German theologian with a fat cigar. Here was a man who had devoted his entire life to the study of God. A man who had sacrificed all and put his life on the line to take a stand for God. And this man was telling me that his value as a person did not come from any of the great things he did for God but from the one great thing the God of the universe did for him. He was loved by God. Therefore, he mattered.

In that brief statement, Dr. Thielicke refocused how I thought of myself. He refocused how I should think of others. That truth has stuck with me for over forty years. Each person is precious because he or she is loved by the Creator of the universe. The apostle John puts it this way: "See what great love the Father has lavished on us, that we should be called children of God! And that is what we are!"[1]

In His great mercy, with so much affection and undeserved grace, God has reaffirmed us as His own. We are children of the Most High God, dearly loved and highly valuable. Our value as human beings has nothing to do with who we are or what we do. Our value as human beings has everything to do with *whose* we are and what *He* does through us.

➤ Mark's Story

According to *Forbes* magazine, there are currently over four hundred billionaires in the United States.[2] Some of them are billionaires several times over. Most of us can't imagine what it would be like to have that much cash. But we wouldn't mind spending a day in their very expensive shoes trying to find out. We are fascinated by the wealthy and the way they spend their money. Of course, what they spend their money on gives us a window into their souls. Some billionaires have been known to purchase huge mansions, rare pieces of artwork, million-dollar yachts, or personal skyscrapers. Billionaire Sir Richard Branson, founder of the Virgin Group, even purchased his own island. It is hard to imagine having that much money, but in reality we are no different than these multibillionaires. How we spend our money, however little we have, still reveals what we value.

In our capitalistic economy, an item's worth is determined by the price that someone is willing to pay for it. We show what we value with our wallets.

When I was two years old, I was put up for auction at the Minnesota State Fair. Let me explain. Somehow I wandered off from my family, probably in search of funnel cakes! Fortunately, someone found me and took me to the auctioneer. My parents were more than a little panicked. Nothing gets your adrenaline pumping like losing your two-year-old in a mob of thousands at a state fair! That's when the auctioneer held me up and took bids. I remind my parents that they had their chance to get rid of me, but evidently they decided to keep me around. They were the top bidders. In fact, they would have emptied their bank account for me! This was one auction they weren't going to lose. No one there that day was going to outbid them. To them, I was priceless.

When a child is lost, everything is narrowed down to one focal point, one mission: finding that child. Every other thing of importance fades into the background until the child is safe in his parents' arms. It's at that moment that the celebration breaks out. Joy unspeakable. The lost has been found.

In Luke, Jesus paints a picture of this taking place in the parable of the lost sheep. He is the Good Shepherd and He sees us, His sheep, as priceless. There are no lengths He won't go to in order to find us. There's no price He wouldn't pay.

> Now the tax collectors and sinners were all gathering around to hear Jesus. But the Pharisees and the teachers of the law muttered, "This man welcomes sinners and eats with them."
>
> Then Jesus told them this parable: "Suppose one of you has a hundred sheep and loses one of them. Doesn't he leave the ninety-nine in the open country and go after the lost sheep until he finds it? And when he finds it, he joyfully puts it on his shoulders and goes home. Then he calls his friends and neighbors together and says, 'Rejoice with me; I have found my lost sheep.' I tell you that in the same way there will be more rejoicing in heaven over one sinner who repents than over ninety-nine righteous persons who do not need to repent."[3]

The Pharisees didn't get Jesus. What was this teacher doing hanging out with a bunch of worthless sinners? Why was He investing in a bunch of religious misfits who didn't know what it meant to be holy? But Jesus sets them straight. He didn't see those people as irredeemable; He saw them as invaluable and irreplaceable. They weren't outcasts; they were offspring. They weren't losers; they were lost. They were His sheep. His Father's lost kids. There is only one thing He is interested in: finding the lost and reuniting them with the Father.

I have learned more about the heavenly Father by becoming an earthly father than I ever did by earning three seminary degrees. The fatherly feelings I have toward my children have helped me understand the way that God feels toward me. The way I love my kids gives me a window into the heart of the heavenly Father. If something happened to Parker, Summer, or Josiah, there is nothing I wouldn't do, no price I wouldn't pay, to set it right. God is no different in the way He feels about you. His love for you is inestimable. He is a Dad on a mission.

It's our misconceptions about God that lead to misconceptions about ourselves. We often act like orphans instead of the adopted children God has chosen. He's more proud of you than you can imagine. And you have no idea how many times you've put a smile on His face. The heavenly Father loves catching His children doing things right. I can picture Him elbowing his angels and saying, "Look, that's my boy" or "That's my girl." The heart of the heavenly Father is revealed at Jesus' baptism.

"This is My beloved Son, in whom I am well pleased."[4]

You are beloved.

There never has been and never will be anyone like you. That is not a testament to you; it is a testament to the God who created you. And it means no one else can worship God *like you* or *for you*. In the eyes of the Creator, you are invaluable and irreplaceable. You are the apple of His eye. There is no price that He is not willing to pay to have a relationship with you. He refuses to be outloved and outdone by anyone. With His death on the cross, Jesus established a price point that was so high no one could outbid Him. The cross says you are worth dying for. The resurrection gives you something worth living for. It's time to start living your life like the highly valued, deeply loved child of God that you are.

No One Can Worship God Like You or For You

10

Holy and Happy

Dick's Story

"Marry and Move" would make a great country song. And it might be decent advice. Ruth and I married in Modesto, California, on a sweltering July night. Three weeks later we drove 2,100 miles to Wheaton, Illinois, for graduate school. Two years apart from family and friends did one thing for us: *it helped us depend on each other*. But my graduate degree didn't help me much at home. I was still a sophomore in marriage.

We were still learning how to love and listen when we returned to California to work with Ruth's dad, Roy Blakeley. Some friends in town started a flying club called the Valley Sky Hawks. Seeing the chance for adventure, I joined up. Asking Ruth what she thought about it didn't really occur to me. I went to ground school and took my first solo flight out of Manteca Airport in a J3 Piper Cub after eleven hours of flying lessons. I was cool. Ruth was not amused.

One day my friend Bill invited me to go up from a nearby farm airstrip in an Aeronca Champ, a tandem-seated, single-engine training plane. Ruth was wary. "I feel like you shouldn't."

"Ruth," I responded, "I'm just going to go up with him for a little while." Men like to think they are logical. What were the odds that something could happen? I had a good solid eleven hours of flying under my belt!

She said, "I just have this sense you shouldn't do that." She was thinking about me and my safety. I was thinking about me and my love of a good adventure.

She rode to the airstrip with me. I got out of the car and said something smooth like, "Woman, go home." Not my best move.

The rest of the story went something like this: Woman went home. Man got in plane. Man crashed on takeoff. Man walked into house twenty minutes later with face white like a sheet.

"What happened?" woman asked.

"We crashed!" Man then proceeded to sob on her shoulder.

I paid a lot more attention after that. Listening to Ruth's feelings and her take on our marriage became one of my top priorities. More than once her words have kept me safe. Relationships never work well when you only listen to yourself.

So often a man speaks his thoughts and his wife speaks her feelings. Trust me, feelings are way deeper. To assume we are on the same communication frequency just because we are talking is to step in a big hole. We need to say whatever it is and then say it again. Then we need to rephrase it and ask, "Did I hear you say . . . ?" or "Did you mean by that . . . ?"

Perhaps we should examine the Navy model in marital talks. We were with some guests on the bridge of the USS *Abraham Lincoln* in Norfolk Harbor some years ago. Our host was explaining how the officer of the deck communicated with the helmsman, in this case a young woman from Colorado who had been in the Navy for just seven months and was nineteen!

It was simply this: An order is given ("Turn twelve degrees to starboard"), and the helmsman repeats it aloud ("Twelve degrees to starboard"). When she has done it, she says, "Twelve degrees to starboard, sir. Heading 210 degrees south southwest." He then repeats, "Current heading 210 degrees south southwest." Apart from the "order" piece, repetition and feedback in a marriage could save time, money, and lonely nights on the couch.

Taking the time to hear a spouse brings honor and credence to the conversation. It acknowledges the value of the other person. If we stop talking or listening, we are dead in the water. Silence in a marriage is not golden. It is ambiguous. When silence falls, I don't know what it means—or am scared I *do* know what it means. Without clear communication, our greatest adventure can become a terrible trip.

My friend Dick Dobbins, a psychologist, says this about marriage: "If it is good, it is incredible. If it is bad, it is incredible!" Marriage has the ability to be the best thing or the worst thing that can happen to us. When communication fails, the latter is guaranteed.

Years ago I did a wedding for a young friend. Six months into the marriage, he came to talk to me.

"How's it going?" I asked.

"Not so good."

"What's the matter?"

"I don't know."

"How are you communicating?"

"Not so good."

"If you aren't communicating," I said, reflecting on my own experience, "then pretty much you have problems with sex, money, and in-laws."

He said, "Bingo, bingo, bingo!"

Sex, money, and in-laws are the points at which we find our identity so often. They are who I am. They are what I bring to the table. When communication breaks down, so do key expressions of the marriage: sexuality, finances, and family.

Sometimes men and women don't communicate well because they interpret life so differently. It's like hearing a foreign language—trying to understand Chinese when you are fluent in Swahili. Both parties are talking, but they certainly don't understand each other. It's the Tower of Babel in our family room.

Sadly, you won't find a CliffsNotes version on how to love and understand each other. God has given you this incredible gift of a person. It's up to you to be curious enough to ask the right questions and then be observant enough to learn how that person needs to be loved. Marriage is meant to be a lifelong journey of discovery.

I often end marriage retreats with a specific exercise. I have the spouses join hands and close their eyes. Then I preface my prayer with this instruction: "Hear what I'm saying. The person whose hand you hold is an original from the land of the Holy Spirit. They are a gift to you to be held in trust, so treat them with grace, with kindness, with mercy, and with respect, because you only get one shot at this deal."

God loves marriage. He designed it. He ordained it. Jesus reflects the Torah when he says it this way: "But at the beginning of creation God 'made them male and female.' 'For this reason a man will leave his father and mother and be united to his wife, and the two will become one flesh.' So they are no longer two, but one flesh. Therefore what God has joined together, let no one separate."[1]

A man leaving his parents in Middle Eastern culture was unheard of. So whatever is suggested here is a really big deal. At the very least it means each of us gives 100 percent, so the cleaving part takes hold. That is serious work, and it guarantees serious reward.

Place the needs and wants and the hopes and dreams of your spouse first. Anything and everything you do with and for the other accrues to a common account that pays huge dividends.

When we think it through, that intention is an act of consecration—a setting apart. The word Scripture uses is *holy*. Not a stuffy, stultified piety. Not a bracketed, law-riddled existence. But an eyes-wide-open investment in the most unique human relationship you will ever enjoy

Your best adventures are yet to come.

Mark's Story

When I married my wife, Lora, I hit the jackpot. She is a great wife, a terrific mom, and my best friend. She is beautiful inside and out. And she likes me. That helps a lot when you are married. Over the two decades we have been married, we have learned a thing or two about relationships. We have learned how to play to our strengths and compensate for each other's weaknesses. We have discovered that adventuring together keeps us connected. And we have found that no matter what, focusing on the other person first is the key to having a great marriage.

Those lessons haven't all come easy. I like to say that we have been happily married for twenty years, but we just celebrated our twenty-second anniversary. You can do the math! Those first two years were rough. We were pretty green when it came to figuring out how to love each other. Mostly because we weren't focusing on loving each other first. We came into our marriage focusing on how we wanted to be loved. Those of you who are married know that self-focused marriages don't do that well.

In Tim Keller's book *The Meaning of Marriage*, he emphasizes that the key to marriage is focusing on meeting the other person's needs. If we are really honest, our unstated goal in getting married is getting our needs met. The problem is that when we start focusing on getting our own needs met, it is a recipe for disappointment, discouragement, and disaster.

Let me tell you what each of us needs in our marriage. Each one of us needs a Copernican revolution. In the sixteenth century, an astronomer by the name of Nicolaus Copernicus made a revolutionary discovery. Up until that point it was assumed by most people that the sun revolved around the earth. But Copernicus's view was heliocentric—he believed the earth actually revolved around the sun. And he was right. Like Copernicus, we need a full-scale revolution—we need to come to terms with the fact that the world doesn't revolve around us! Marriage is about giving instead of getting. And that is the difference between lust and love. Lust focuses on getting what it wants. Love focuses on giving what it has. If we find true joy in loving that person the way they need to be loved, we are setting ourselves up for an amazing journey.

The goal of marriage is not happiness, it is holiness. That thought is not original to me, but I have experienced it firsthand. There is no mechanism whereby God can sanctify a person more than having them live in close proximity to another imperfect person. When I get into an emotional slump, nine times out of ten it's because I zoom in on something I'm not happy about and I need to zoom out and refocus on something I'm grateful for. In the same sense, when I get into a relational slump, nine times out of ten it's because I zoom in on getting my needs met and I need to zoom out and refocus on meeting someone else's needs. If the goal of marriage is just to be happy all the time, and not a process of God sanctifying us, then we run into trouble. We don't end up sanctified or happy. We usually end up dissatisfied and desperate.

Our fundamental problem is that we are selfish. Marriage is the means whereby God eradicates our selfishness because it is not about "me" anymore, it is about "we." Of course, some of us need a little more eradication than others. So God gives us kids! And it usually takes more than one kid to do the job! Marriage is meant to be a joint venture. And by that, I don't mean a 50-50 proposition. It's 100-100. When you know someone is in your corner till death do you part, it gives you the courage to go another round. It's *us* against the world.

Early on in our marriage, Lora and I started discovering what each one of us was good at and not good at. When we first got married, she kept our checkbook and tracked our finances. Then I decided that I would give it a shot. Honestly, how hard could it be? All you do is get the monthly bank statement and reconcile the total. I didn't realize it was slightly more complicated than that. That experiment lasted for one whole month! Lora is, hands down, the best checkbook reconciler in the family. I submit to her checkbook-keeping skills. I, on the other hand, handle most of our investments. I excel at the big picture, and she excels in the fine print. She trusts me to manage our overall investments, and I trust her to manage our monthly cash flow.

A good marriage is like learning to tango without stepping on each other's toes. There is a give-and-take, honoring and submitting, that gives beauty to the dance. We live in a culture where the word *submission* has fallen out of favor, probably because of malpractice. But if it's done right, it makes for a strong marriage. Submission doesn't mean giving up and giving in. It simply means *to yield the right of way*. Submission is the art of compensating for your weaknesses by playing to each other's strengths.

When I officiate weddings, I offer a simple piece of advice: *never forget why you fell in love in the first place*. Not only do we need to remember, we need to call it out. And we need to do it both publicly and privately. To cherish is to out-love, out-care, out-share, and out-give each other. It revolutionizes the way we see life. It sanctifies our selfish nature. It opens up our eyes to what true love really looks like, and when we get it right, we get in on the adventure of a lifetime.

Happiness Is a By-Product of Holiness

11

Playing for Keeps

Dick's Story

One hundred fifty thousand of anything is a huge number. When that is the number of soldiers going into battle, it is staggering.

On a blustery gray morning in June of 1944, that many young men charged onto fifty miles of beach in the north of France. Some of them, paratroopers, had dropped out of the sky during the night and were already scattered among the hedgerows. The boys who landed there, so many of them teenagers, felt one emotion: stark terror. More than two thousand of them would never see another sunrise. Deliverance for Europe from the clutches of Nazi Germany would be bought at a dear price.

In June of 2012, the weather on Utah Beach in Normandy was not much different. Wind whipped waves into froth as gulls screeched and dove. The sun was lost behind dark clouds. A light drizzle dampened our sweatshirts. But the emotion I felt standing on that sacred sand was totally different. Gratitude. Gratitude for the sacrifice that bought freedom for millions. And gratitude for the young man standing with me: my grandson, Sam.

Being a grandparent makes me feel immortal. I get to go beyond the next generation. At this writing, Ruth and I have eleven grandchildren ages five to twenty-three. We echo all grandparents in the world when we think our grandchildren are bright, funny, engaging, and unique. Most of our grandkids live in other states, and we are intentional about spending time with them. To see them grow and excel is great joy. To see them run their folks ragged is cosmic payback.

My sense of family comes a great deal from Ruth. For her, there is no higher impetus for living, apart from knowing Jesus, than family. She has often said, "All I ever wanted to be was a mother and a grandmother." She has mastered both.

In her early years she grew up living around the corner from her mother's parents on a farm just north of Modesto, California. When her parents moved to Portland, Oregon, after her first grade year, they made sure the family ties stayed tight. Each summer she and her two brothers, John and Phil, made the trek back to the farm to stay with Grandma and Grandpa Presnell. Those months—months of heaven—shaped her soul. Playing in the orchards with cousins. Baking with Grandma. Feeding chickens with Grandpa. Summer on the farm is Ruth's model for what grandparents are about.

In our early grandparenting years, Ruth and I set two goals: to track the big journey and to take a small journey. She tracked the big journey by keeping a journal for each grandchild. For the past twenty-two years each time she has been with one of them, she writes notes about what they have talked about, what they made, where they went, and what games they played. It is a treasure and a testament.

When Alyson, our oldest grandchild, graduated from high school, she was presented with "Grandma's Journal," a pictorial book of Aly at different ages with drawings from her preschool and elementary years, punctuated by notes Ruth had written about her over the last eighteen years. Our second grandchild, Claire, received hers in the summer of 2013. She took it with her to her graduation party so all her friends could check it out.

The small journey was, literally, a journey. We decided that if we had the physical and economic capacity, we would take each grandchild on a trip when they reached the age of thirteen, as a rite of passage, like Mark has done with his own children. The summer that Alyson turned thirteen, I was invited to speak at a conference in Spain. She came with us. When Claire turned thirteen, she came with us to Scotland and England. Their brother, our third grandchild, Sam, is a World War II buff. When he was twelve, he and his dad, Van, started researching World War II in Europe. Normandy was a metaphor for the whole war. At thirteen, he was ready.

Sam, Van, and I flew to London from Portland, Oregon, on June 9 and spent a day touring the city with special attention to the Churchill War Rooms. Taking in the sights and sounds of the city by tour boat on the Thames River, we hopped off to go exploring and ended up near Lincoln's Inn Fields. Hundreds of people were milling about in the Saturday afternoon sunshine.

A church group was having a festival in the square. Listening to the band and watching the brightly dressed folks passing out literature, our attention soon shifted to the sound of bells ringing. Bike bells. As we looked over our shoulders, bicyclists without shirts began rounding the corner. As they pulled onto the straightaway, we saw that the shirtless bikers were also pantsless! Hundreds of naked bicyclists rode past us. We had come face-to-face with London's World Wide Naked Bike Ride. Van and I said something like, "Sam! Eyes on the worship band!" The alternative wasn't pretty.

Early the next morning we boarded a train for Southampton, a D-Day launch point. Taking the ferry across the English Channel, we approached the Normandy coast as dawn lit the eastern sky. Trying to imagine the feelings of an eighteen-year-old in a Higgins landing craft churning for five miles through choppy waters on that world-altering June morning in 1944, I couldn't come close.

Our lodgings were six miles inland from the beach at the Chateau de Vouilly, where a cluster of United States news reporters had stayed for three months after the Normandy landings. They lived in tents on the sprawling lawn. As Allied troops battled through the treacherous French hedgerows, Ernie Pyle, Andy Rooney, and Walter Cronkite recorded history on battered typewriters at the same tables where we sat eating our breakfast of hot chocolate and baguettes.

Sam was as enamored of the French cuisine as he was of the rich layers of history. Each meal required a reverential picture to be taken, from buttery croissants in Normandy to Nutella crepes from a street vendor in Paris. Van and I chronicled our trip by historic sites visited, and Sam chronicled our trip by great meals eaten. It was a fantastic trip all the way around. We went home with a wealth of memories and full bellies to boot.

Sam absorbed each day through his pores. Stuffing our faces with croissants, dashing for a tour boat on the Thames, and sweating as we climbed the iron stairs of the Eiffel Tower created a kaleidoscope of memory. And I suppose it helped this grandpa to be a child one more time.

Psalm 127:3 says, "Children are a gift from the LORD; they are a reward from him" (NLT). Ruth and I know this to be true in a hundred different ways. Each moment spent with our kids and grandkids comes back to us pressed down, shaken together, and poured into our lap.

The apostle Paul ramps it up further when he says to his spiritual son, Timothy, "I am reminded of your sincere faith, which first lived in your grandmother Lois and in your mother Eunice and, I am persuaded, now lives in you also."[1]

This past Christmas, Sam gave me my own pictorial memoir of our trip, one of those hardcover Shutterfly-type books. It is what his sisters had done after their trips. Sam's book was filled with pictures of places, people, and food from our Normandy adventure, minus the infamous bicyclists. Inscribed on the back cover it says:

A trip of a lifetime. This was the greatest experience of my entire life. I'm so happy to have been able to do it with my Grandpa and my Dad. These would be my two go-to guys to travel the world with. Thank you, Grandpa, for taking us and for such a wonderful adventure. Love you the most, Samuel.

I read those words and could hardly stand it. I grinned and welled up at the same moment. After seventy-two trips around the sun, that paragraph was a sweet, unexpected, delightful payoff.

Mark's Story

When you are playing marbles as a kid, you can either play for funsies or you can play for keeps. When your kids are little, parenting is like playing for funsies because young children are very forgetful, very forgiving. They won't even remember the mistakes you made! I honestly believe that God intentionally created us in such a way that we don't remember the first few years of life. That is one of His greatest acts of grace, because who would want to remember having their diaper changed!

By the way, the word *diaper* spelled backwards is *repaid*. Just saying.

Once your kids get older, parenting is like playing for keeps. The stakes get higher. You realize that your words can carry the weight of the world. Now, just to take a little pressure off, let me share something Lora shared with me on one of our Monday coffee dates. She said, "You think our kids will follow Jesus *because of* us. I think they'll follow Jesus *in spite of* us." Once again, I think Lora is right. That one revelation took so much pressure off of me. At the same time, I believe that the way we love our kids can help shape their identity. Who they become is a reflection of the time and energy you've poured into them. As they round the corner on the teenage years, you start counting down the number of years they have under your roof. You realize that your time together is precious. It's our job to make every moment count.

My friend Reggie Joiner actually encourages parents to buy a large glass jar and fill it with 936 marbles. That's 1 marble times 52 weeks times 18 years. It's a countdown clock of sorts. Each week, parents remove one marble as a reminder that they are *playing for keeps* (which, by the way, is the title of the book he's written on the subject). It's a healthy reminder of the old adage: *the days are long but the years are short*.

Lora and I had been married three years when our first child, Parker, was born. We got married young and started our family young. That meant we had way more energy, but the tradeoff was that we didn't have much wisdom. I can't recount the number of times I had a crisis counseling session with Foth on the subject of marriage or parenting. He reminded me more than once of a simple biblical truth: *this too shall pass*. Sometimes the most spiritual thing you can do is just hang in there. Then hang in there a little longer! For the record, one of the tricks of the trade that I picked up from Foth is that he never asks me how I'm doing first. He always says, "How are Lora and the kids?" He knows that how they're doing will give him a good gauge on how I'm doing!

We really didn't have any idea what we were doing as parents, but we decided to have a few more kids to have more fun. Summer and Josiah completed our family, and there was no looking back. With three kids, your energy is divided by three, but your joy is multiplied by three. Our early years of parenting were like controlled chaos. We felt equally blessed and stressed, loving the opportunity to be parents to these three unique kids.

As Parker began to edge toward adolescence, the urgency that Lora and I felt about parenting him with intentionality multiplied. We began to realize that we were playing for keeps, and our greatest legacy wouldn't be the church we pastored or the books I wrote. Our greatest legacy will be our three children: Parker, Summer, and Josiah.

When our kids hit their teenage years, we had dinner with some long-tenured pastors in the DC area. John and Susan Yates, pastors of The Falls Church, were sharing how they were trying to invest in their grandkids. John said having grandchildren was a great moment of revelation that life really is about the legacy you leave in your children and grandchildren. Each year John and Susan hold a cousins camp for their twenty-one grandkids on their farm. They spend a week making memories and building relationships. I want to parent my kids with the same kind of creativity and intentionality. And just for the record, one of the ways God redeems the mistakes we make as parents is by allowing us a second chance, called grandparenting. Dick has mentored me as a father by sharing some of his deepest regrets, but I also see the way he has channeled those regrets into a renewed desire to be an even better grandfather than father.

Before Parker turned twelve, I knew I wanted to do a yearlong discipleship covenant to prepare him to become a teenager. To prepare myself I read quite a few books, including *Raising a Modern-Day Knight* by Robert Lewis, which was a great help. I asked different dads what they had done with their sons to commemorate this important season in life. And then I jumped in.

I spent several months creating a discipleship covenant. It had an intellectual, spiritual, and physical component to it. The intellectual component was that we would read one book a month. Those books ranged from fiction to nonfiction, including *The Purpose Driven Life* by Rick Warren and a book or two that I had written. I wanted to inculcate the love of reading, and Parker is now a voracious reader. He reads way beyond his grade level, and I would like to take a little credit for that. I also think his reading habit has helped cultivate his writing ability—Parker has coauthored three books for teens with me.[2]

The second piece was the physical covenant. We trained for and completed a sprint triathlon together, which was wonderful fun. It was great going after a goal together.

The spiritual dimension was multifaceted. We did a number of different things, including reading through the New Testament and fasting from television for Lent. We came up with his life goal list and included that in the covenant as well. We signed the covenant on his twelfth birthday, and then on his thirteenth birthday, we went and hiked the Grand Canyon from rim to rim as a rite of passage. We wanted to do something together that would be very challenging. That investment will pay dividends until the day I die, but it will also pay dividends long after that. The memories we forged during that year were unforgettable. I also believe it's a multigenerational blessing that will be passed on to the third and fourth generation.

At a formative stage in his life, Parker got the best I had to offer. I wish I could say that about all my kids all the time. But I knew I needed to seize that window of opportunity to invest in his life. The investment I made in Parker is probably one of the most significant things I've done—far more important than writing a book or pastoring a church. This year I'm doing it all over again with Josiah. It looks different because Josiah is different. It's tailored to his unique gifts and passions.

Sometimes we are given a revelation of what is truly important in life. For me, one of those moments happened while traveling through an airport during a very busy season of life. I was speaking at so many conferences that I had a hard time keeping track of what time zone I was in. Those speaking opportunities were the by-product of God's blessing—a church that was growing and books that were touching people's lives. But the blessing can easily become a curse if you don't manage it right. After all, mismanaged success is the leading cause of failure! As I ran toward my gate, it was like a switch flipped in my soul. I realized that my occupational achievements were meaningless if I had to sacrifice my family on the altar of ministry.

I had to come to grips with the answers to a few soul-searching questions. Was I giving my most important moments and the best of myself to those I cared about the most? Or was I investing most of my time in relationships that wouldn't endure past my next book release? It was an issue of stewardship. Without my family, none of these accomplishments means anything. That's when a little saying became a heartfelt mantra: *I want to be famous in my home.* I also came up with a definition of success: *success is when those who know you best respect you most.*

Lora and I work hard at playing for keeps with our kids. We want to look back on these years with Parker, Summer, and Josiah as years where we gave the best of ourselves to the ones we love best of all. We may not be perfect in our parenting, but we want to be present. We want to know we were good stewards of the greatest gifts God has given us: our kids. You may not be the parent you want to be, but today can be the day you realize that your children are your legacy. You can begin to love them with purpose and intentionality. You can be famous in your own home. And that's what matters most. You can determine the richness of your life by how much you invest in those you love. And whatever you do, don't wait another minute to start playing for keeps.

───────────────✦───────────────

Don't Sacrifice Your Family on the Altar of Success

12

Never a Dull Moment

Is loving God solely an introspective journey? Is it just for mystics? My friend Anna, who spent three lifetimes in a land filled with mystics, would likely say, "No!"

Rupaidiha, northern India, is nothing like Dayton, Ohio.

Anna Tomaseck, a nurse from Dayton, sailed to India in 1924 in response to a call made by an older woman to rescue abandoned and orphaned children on the border of Nepal. At twenty-four, her whole life lay ahead. The move meant she would leave all she knew and break her engagement to a young medical student, knowing she might never marry.

It was not a woman's world. Women had only had the vote in the United States since 1920. Women in India had far fewer rights than that. To do what she did at the time she did it was more than bold. Some thought she was foolish. Others thought she wouldn't last. But she had come to stay. Anna had thrown off a safe life as her way of "loving God with all her heart." The challenge from that older woman missionary was the gauntlet thrown down. Her world had turned inside out.

When Ruth and I met Anna, known then as Mama Ji ("respected mother"), at a gathering in Bangalore, India, in the early seventies, we became friends. We had the India connection, we had the adventuring connection, and I loved hearing her stories. When I became president at Bethany College, I knew our students needed to meet her. An eightyish woman who was passionate, engaging, and inspirational? Of course they had to meet her.

We didn't need talks from Mama Ji. We needed conversations with her. Our students, young and on the cusp of the real world, were getting to see and hear firsthand a life poured out in love to Jesus. She regaled us with stories of mission and of miracles: The moment, during one sleep-deprived night of feeding infants, when the Spirit roused her just in time to save a baby from a rat that had crawled into her crib. The time her lap dogs saved her when a king cobra coiled in the lattice on her porch struck and barely missed, as they tugged her back by the hem of her dressing gown. And she told stories of child after unwanted child responding to the love of Jesus seen in a white woman. They grew to love Him back.

On the final morning of her time with us, I asked her, in front of the students, "What would be an incident that you would see as a metaphor for all those decades in India?" Following is the story she told.

Early one morning Anna heard a banging on the door of her home, where at the time she and a co-worker cared for twenty-three children. She opened the door to see a man standing with a bundle in his arms. The bundle was a newborn baby girl. With no sewer system in the village, the man had gone out to the village dung heap early in the morning to relieve himself when he saw some movement beneath leaves at the base of a tree. When he brushed away the leaves, he found a newborn baby girl with umbilical cord and placenta still attached. At that time in that culture, baby girls were disposable. She had been born to some travelers coming through the area at night and thrown away to die. The man brought her to Anna because he knew that she would care for her. Mama Ji, the respected mother, and her co-worker did just that.

They kept her until the age of seven when she was adopted by a wealthy family in New Delhi. Over the next twenty years they heard from her occasionally. Then one day a letter from her arrived with a photograph enclosed. The letter had been posted in London, England, and it told this story.

The parents discovered that their adopted daughter had a gift for music, so they gave her piano lessons. By the time she was sixteen, she was so proficient on the piano that her parents sent her to the London Conservatory of Music. The picture in the envelope was that girl, now twenty-seven, sitting with the royal family following a concert she had given at Buckingham Palace.

It is a long way from a dung heap in a remote Indian village to high tea at Buckingham Palace. And it is a long way from a broken engagement in Dayton, Ohio, to bringing up four hundred kids for God on the border of Nepal.

Loving God is not just for contemplatives. Loving God is laying down your life in service to the Creator so that He can give it back to you.

When we decide that our lives are about that kind of loving, the journey begins. It changes our trajectory. It helps us see another's trash as God's treasure. It might send us to the other side of the street or to the other side of the earth.

Anna's life was not easy, and her love for Jesus was not an add-on. The spaces between the miracles were long and hard as she poured her heart and life into children that other people had written off. There were disappointments that left her weary and diseases that left her weak. There were days of little food for the children and nights of prayer vigils at the beds of sick babies. She answered Jesus' call and invested fifty-two years in a place with a name she'd never heard until she was twenty-four. She had come face-to-face with the words of Jesus:

> I was hungry and you gave me something to eat, I was thirsty and you gave me something to drink, I was a stranger and you invited me in, I needed clothes and you clothed me. . . . Whatever you did for *one of the least of these brothers and sisters of mine, you did for me*.[1]

How do we love God? One way is to love the world's discarded like Anna did. The disabled and disconnected. The diseased and disenfranchised. The displaced and the disallowed. Those who are categorically or specifically "dissed."

On that night in Bangalore when we first met Anna at a south Indian seminary, she answered the call again. She was sitting toward the back of the chapel when the speaker at the close of his message waved to her and said, "Anna, if you would give fifty-two years to Jesus and India again, please come down to the front."

Suffering from the early stages of elephantiasis, a condition caused by parasites blocking the flow of lymphatic fluid in the body, she shuffled down the aisle on swollen, slippered feet. As she limped by us with tears streaming down her face, I heard her murmur, "I'd do it a million times. I'd do it a million times. I'd do it a million times!"

To follow Jesus is the epic adventure. It turns us inside out. It blazes trails. It yields miracles. It redeems and restores. It costs everything. It gives the greatest reward. Anna found that out in Dayton, as a nurse, and in Rupadiah, as Mama Ji. We will not have Anna's journey, of course. But we will have our own.

And if we get it right and have the chance to do it again? We'd do it a million times!

Mark's Story

When I was five years old, our family went to see a Billy Graham Evangelistic Association film called *The Hiding Place*. The plotline of that movie changed the plotline of my life. Corrie ten Boom and her family were sent to a concentration camp for hiding their Jewish friends in their home during the Nazi occupation of Holland. After losing her father and sister in the camp, Corrie was released by a clerical error. Corrie went on to change the world, and change my life, with her message of forgiveness. The movie wasn't usual viewing for a five-year-old because it was a very graphic depiction of the concentration camps. But somehow that movie pulled at my heartstrings.

Later that night, when my mom was tucking me into bed, I asked her if I could ask Jesus into my heart. We prayed together, and my journey with Jesus began. During my childhood and high school years, my concept of following Jesus was more about my agenda for Him than His agenda for me. Whatever I was doing, He was welcome to come along. I invited Jesus to follow me into the classroom and onto the basketball court and help me do what I wanted to do. But it was more about God serving my purposes than me serving His.

My true spiritual revolution happened when I was nineteen. It's not that I wasn't saved when I was five or that I didn't love God when I was a kid. I had an understanding of the cross and what Christ had done for me, but it was a selfish spirituality up until that point. The defining moment for me came when I began to seek the Lord in college. I would go up in the balcony of our chapel and pray during lunch every day. My prayers began to be less about telling God what I wanted Him to do for me. I began asking Him what I could do for Him. That's when the true adventure began. My life began to change. My heart began to change. And my desires began to shift.

Most people are bored with their faith because they are selfish. They think they are following Jesus, but the reality is that they have invited Jesus to follow them. They are trying to *lead* instead of accepting the invitation to *follow*. I call it the inverted gospel. And it's absolutely unfulfilling. It's not until you say to God "whatever, whenever, wherever" that you begin living out the adventure God has planned for you. Trust me, you cannot follow Jesus and be bored at the same time!

I have a conviction that church should be anything but boring. Part of that deeply held desire is undoubtedly a reaction to some of the churches our family went to while I was growing up. No church is perfect, and I certainly don't want to throw the baby out with the bathwater. But some of the churches we went to were so legalistic you would think smiling was a sin. And laughter was the unforgivable sin! It's like they were designed to be as unenjoyable as possible. For many people, church is the most monotonous hour of the week, void of emotion. And the tragedy is that people equate that deadpan sentiment with following Jesus.

One of the lessons I've learned from Dick is that great sermons are the by-product of great stories, which are the by-product of great lives. I had next to no life experience when I started preaching, so I had to beg, borrow, and steal from illustration books. Then I would listen to Dick preach, and you could tell his sermons didn't originate in a book well studied. They originated in a life well lived. His stories touched the deepest emotions—they made people laugh and cry in the same sermon. And the element of adventure always caused a surge of adrenaline that made me want to drop my nets all over again and follow Jesus wherever He would lead me!

We so quickly and so easily lose sight of what's really important in life. In the words of Stephen Covey, "Anything less than a conscious commitment to the important is an unconscious commitment to the unimportant."[2] And before we know it, we're majoring in minors and minoring in majors. That's why Jesus kept going back to the Great Commandment. He reduced the 613 Old Testament laws into one common denominator: "Love the Lord your God with all your heart and with all your soul and with all your mind and with all your strength."[3]

If we're going to be *great* at something, let's be great at the Great Commandment. If that is what matters most, then it had better be the focal point of our lives. I've had the privilege of not just hearing messages about the Great Commandment but seeing it modeled in the life of a spiritual father. I've never met anyone who loves people more than Dick Foth does, and that's what happens when you love Jesus above all.

I don't think Corrie ten Boom set out to live her life as an adventure. She was simply trying to survive a horrific tragedy. But that didn't keep her from loving God with all her heart, soul, mind, and strength. She said, "We never know how God will answer our prayers, but we can expect that He will get us involved in His plan for the answer. If we are true intercessors, we must be ready to take part in God's work on behalf of the people for whom we pray."[4] You are someone else's miracle! Corrie ten Boom's plan was to be an apprentice in her father's work. She wanted to be a watchmaker. God's plan was for Corrie ten Boom to be an apprentice in her heavenly Father's work. He wanted her to be a history changer. She went from being a prisoner of war in a German death camp to being a beacon of forgiveness and hope in war-torn Germany. She went from living out the first forty-eight years of her life in the same childhood bedroom of her father's home to traveling the world, spreading a message of light and life to millions. One thing is for sure:

Corrie ten Boom may have been scared, anxious, brave, courageous, wounded, triumphant, weak, powerful, desperate, and hope filled . . . but she was never bored.

True Greatness Is Being Great
at the Great Commandment

13

The Five-and-a-Half-Inch World between Your Ears

Dick's Story

"As a Jew in Budapest, did you have to wear one of those yellow stars?"

This was my question of the old gentleman who joined us for lunch that Sunday afternoon in Queens, New York. He had been raised in Budapest, Hungary, in the 1930s and 1940s. When the Nazis took the city in 1944, he was a teenager. After a time they sent him to a forced labor camp. He escaped twice and was recaptured. Finally they sent him to Auschwitz, the place that has become a metaphor for demonic atrocity. By tenacity and some miracles, he lived and was liberated by the Allies in 1945.

After listening to his story, I asked if he had to wear one of those yellow stars. He just grinned at me and said, "Oh no, I was never good enough to get a star!" I laughed with hesitation at his gallows humor. His next words jarred me. Stone-cold serious, he said, "I made up my mind that if anybody walked out of the camps alive, it was going to be me." I was not speaking with a survivor. I was speaking with a victor.

When Scripture says, "As a man thinks, so is he,"[1] it is raw truth. How we approach life and react to its vagaries determines the bulk of our character. How we love is locked into how we think about it. What angers us is triggered by how we think. It is between our ears that we decide how easily offended we will be. When it comes to harsh words from others, whether my skin absorbs like cotton or deflects like Teflon is a decision I make. All of that happens in a three-pound organ five-and-a-half inches across called my brain. In a very real sense, my world begins and ends between my ears. I don't have to be brain-dead to be brain-defeated.

In 1997, Roberto Benigni directed and starred in *Life Is Beautiful*, which won three Oscars. It is a take-your-breath-away story of a poor Jewish watchmaker who marries his Italian love, and they have a little boy. When the boy is five, the Nazis come to their village, and father and son are sent to a concentration camp. To save his boy, the father makes the gruesome journey into a game. The game does just that. It saves him. And it all started with a father's decision.

If from the outset we decide that life is not just meant to be survived, we will experience adventure at every turn—in every person we meet, every relationship we have, every book we read. If we believe life is an adventure, life is an adventure. If we believe we will make it through great trials, we will most often make it through great trials. If we believe that there is joy to be had each day of our lives, we will have it.

This is not a new thought. Certainly not an original thought. It is an eternal truth that begs for mulling and musing. It deserves to be treasured deep in the heart. Mark and I have reflected on this idea a lot. Flying home from a speaking engagement in 1992,

I watched Hugh Downs on a *20/20* clip. He was interviewing folks from one of the fastest-growing population subgroups in the United States: people who had lived more than a hundred years. At that time there were 36,000 centenarians in this country. A study had been done to see what, if anything, these aging-but-vital people had in common.[2] The researchers found four qualities: (1) optimism, (2) engagement, (3) mobility, and (4) the ability to adapt to loss. This quartet of practices shaped the way they lived out their days.

Two interviews stood out to me in particular. The first was with an avid churchgoing African American gentleman from Georgia named Jesse Champion. "Jesse endured years of back-breaking labor as a sharecropper. His father was a slave. Jesse himself can remember the cruelty of men who treated him, as a young man, as if he were a slave," Hugh Downs commented. "The Lord let me live to see all of 'em dead. Everyone that treated me bad. I outlived them. Yes I did!" Jesse observed. Hugh Downs ended the interview with the question, Are you born again? "Yessuh, I know I'm born again . . . He changed my heart," Champion affirmed.

The most touching interview was with Mary Elliott, a 102-year-old woman whose 77-year-old daughter, Josephine, had died the previous night of a heart attack. Asked if she wished to postpone the time with Hugh Downs, she chose to proceed, partly as a tribute to her daughter. She told Hugh that one of her fondest memories of Josephine was a time when she laid her in her crib as a little girl. Josephine put her head on her pillow and said, "Now, dear God, let's go to sleep." Mrs. Elliott explained that she had been asked to give back to God the gift He had given her, just as quietly and beautifully as her toddler had prayed that seven-word prayer. That's how she decided to deal with her loss. It was in the five-and-a-half inches between her ears that Mary absorbed the pain and made a decision.

The quality of our decisions gives our lives meaning. The decisions that focus us outward provide texture and substance to our lives. Interestingly, one of the takeaways found from these interviews—part of a study conducted in Georgia—was that people live longer when they decide to become passionately involved in something beyond themselves.

What a way these folks looked at life: not focused on tragedy but focused on the One who loved them most. In the face of sorrow and heartbreak, their belief in a loving God stamped their feelings and how they viewed their circumstances.

If indeed the five-and-a-half-inch world where I spend all of my days determines the impact of an eighty- or ninety- or one-hundred-year life, the real question is obvious: *What am I thinking?*

Second

Mark's Story

When Parker turned sixteen, I took him skeet shooting. Before they'd let us onto the shooting range, we had to take a safety class. One of the things the instructor taught us was that we each have a dominant eye. In case you care, I'm right-eyed. So I close my left eye when I shoot. If I closed the wrong eye, I'd have a tough time hitting the clay pigeons. And what's true of skeet shooting is true of life.

Matthew 6:22–23 says, "Your eye is a lamp that provides light for your body. When your eye is good, your whole body is filled with light. But when your eye is bad, your whole body is filled with darkness" (NLT).

We don't see the world as it is; we see the world as we are. As a pastor, I've seen this play out over and over again in the lives of the people around me. I've learned that if someone has a critical eye, they will always find something to be critical about. And if they have a grateful eye, they will find something to celebrate even in the worst of circumstances. The Bible calls this having a "good eye." Having a "good eye" in life changes how you see yourself and everything around you. We have a core value in our family that we borrowed from Qui-Gon Jinn's conversation with Anakin Skywalker: *your focus determines your reality*. We want to have a "good eye" as we walk through life. We want our reality to reflect the good things we choose to focus on. One way I do it is by keeping a gratitude journal. That's how I count God's blessings. I literally number them. Year to date, I'm on #471. My goal is to hit a thousand by year's end.

In Philippians 4:8, Paul says, "Finally, brothers and sisters, whatever is true, whatever is noble, whatever is right, whatever is pure, whatever is lovely, whatever is admirable—if anything is excellent or praiseworthy—think about such things." In other words, focus on those positives. Paul had a lot of painful memories he could have focused on. Over the course of his ministry he was jailed, placed under house arrest, shipwrecked, bitten by a poisonous snake, stoned and left for dead, and whipped at least 195 times. If anyone had a right to feel sorry for themselves, it was probably Paul. Yet he didn't. He chose to focus on the things that would get him where he needed to go. And he encouraged the people around him to keep their eyes focused on the prize, eternity with Christ.[3] It kept him positive. It kept him moving forward. It kept him motivated.

Part of discovering the adventure God has designed you for is learning how to frame it or reframe it. How do you frame experiences, frame opportunities, frame situations? Do you have a "good eye" or a "bad eye"? Martin Seligman, the former president of the American Psychological Association, said that each of us has an explanatory style. Simply put, our explanatory style is how we explain our experiences to ourselves. And our explanation is more important than the experience itself. In the words of Aldous Huxley, "Experience is not what happens to a man; it is what a man does with what happens to him."[4]

When you frame a picture, the color of the frame determines the focus. If you use a gold frame, it'll accentuate the gold in the picture. When it comes to life, you can use a positive frame or negative frame. And it makes all the difference in the world. Joseph may be the best example. He reframed thirteen years of pain and suffering with one explanation. He said to the same brothers who sold him into slavery and left him for dead, "You intended to harm me, but God intended it for good to accomplish what is now being done, the saving of many lives." That statement in Genesis 50:20 is Joseph's explanatory style. Even in bad circumstances, Joseph had a good eye. The key? Keeping your eyes on the promises of God.

One of my favorite "reframes" is said to have happened during the Battle of the Bulge in December 1944. It was a turning point in World War II. American forces were completely surrounded at Bastogne, Belgium. The situation looked hopeless. Our troops were low on morale and even lower on supplies. The German field commander sent a message to General Anthony McAuliffe demanding his immediate surrender. General McAuliffe is purported to have assembled his troops and said, "Men, we are surrounded by the enemy. We have the greatest opportunity ever presented an army. We can attack in any direction."

Over the years Dick has helped me frame some of my greatest challenges and biggest dreams. With a few well-timed words, I've experienced paradigm shifts that have changed the way I view my life. Some of them have been the result of intense conversations, while others have been the by-product of his sense of humor. We haven't always seen eye to eye on absolutely everything, but when your hearts are in alignment, that's okay.

Jesus was the master of reframing things. In a sense, His life on earth was a death march to Calvary's cross, and He knew it. But He didn't live out His days downcast and depressed. He was full of life, full of joy, full of healing, full of wisdom. He lived a life that was so mesmerizing that everyone around Him wanted to be with Him and be like Him. He reframed death into abundant life. He reframed sorrow into joy. He reframed despair into hope everlasting. Ultimately, He reframed death into resurrection. He showed us what a life of adventure truly looked like, and He did it with an eternal frame. He was faced with the dark night of the cross, but He saw Easter morning. And the empty tomb reframes everything.

On July 23, 2000, a near-death experience completely reframed the rest of my life. My intestines ruptured and I was on a respirator for two days. The fact that I survived is no small miracle. In an instant, things that I had taken for granted became precious. After several surgeries and several weeks in the hospital, I knew I should have died in the operating room. I remember walking into my kids' rooms and staring at them as they slept. I realized I had taken not just my kids and my wife but my life for granted in so many different ways. But the worst day of my life turned into the best day of my life because I finally discovered that every day is a gift from God. Stop and think about it: today is the *first day* and *last day* of your life. It never has been before and it never will be again. When you have that revelation, you number your days.[5] You try to make every day a masterpiece.

Make Every Day a Masterpiece

14

Books with Skin Covers

➤ Dick's Story

It was a Sunday morning in March 1969 in Urbana, Illinois. A young man rushed up to me at the close of the service and said, "Do you know who that man was?"

"No idea," I said.

"I work for him," the young man replied. "That was *the* Howard Malmstadt." He and his wife had slipped into the back row of our little colonial-style church after the service began and left during the closing prayer.

I said, "Great! Who is *the* Howard Malmstadt?"

He said, "He is one of the top five spectroscopists in the world!"

I said, "Fantastic! What's a spectroscopist?"

He said, "Those are people who use light for scientific measurement." My education was about to begin.

Howard Malmstadt, I found out, was a legend in the world of chemistry. When World War II interrupted his studies at the

University of Wisconsin, he enlisted as a United States naval radar officer. The Navy introduced him to state-of-the-art electronics. After the war, he brought together chemistry and electronics and began teaching scientists in all disciplines how to collect scientific data through electronics.

By the time I met him, he had written nine textbooks used in over five hundred universities around the world and received the highest international awards for his research. He was widely considered the father of modern electronic and computerized instrumentation in chemistry. His initials, H.V., were morphed by his colleagues into "High Voltage" Malmstadt because of his powerful insights and enthusiastic hands-on teaching. His PhD students and their students would go on to change the face of analytical chemistry. Many were stunned when he left the University of Illinois in 1978 at the peak of his career to become provost of an innovative global university in Kona, Hawaii, called the University of the Nations, an institution that is committed to making known the person of Jesus on the platform of spiritual, cultural, and professional training.

When he showed up that Sunday, I had no idea that his friendship would change my life. It is no small thing when a world-famous scientist chooses you as a friend. We would have breakfast and I would ask questions. I would visit his lab with its banks of computers and bright graduate students standing in line to ask him questions. When I asked about one of his table-top experiments, he said, "That's a ruby laser tracking positive and negative ions across the kidneys of frogs, Dick." Clueless, I nodded knowingly. Though I could barely fathom Howard Malmstadt's world, we brought something to each other. As we grew in our friendship, one thing became clear: he was on a spiritual journey, and I was too.

An incident in his naval career was a turning point in Howard's life. In the last year of the war, the destroyer on which he

131

served was part of a picket line off the coast of Japan. They were under constant threat of kamikaze attack, and the tension was unbearable. After a very hard seventy-two hours at battle stations, he went to his bunk exhausted. Lying there, he heard a voice outside his porthole saying, "The Lord is my shepherd; I shall not want . . ." Brought up in a Presbyterian home, he knew the twenty-third psalm. Howard got up and looked out. No one was there. He told me that moment changed him.

My talks with Howard changed me. One day while riding to lunch, I asked him, "Why do you think the very first thing God says in Genesis is 'Let there be light'?"

He said, "Well, it is one of the foundations of the universe. The speed of light is the constant in Einstein's general theory of relativity, $E = mc^2$. Light is expressed in wavelengths. The most precise unit of measurement for distance is the wavelength. So contractors who build roads use laser transits. Every element on the chart of elements that we study in high school science (Cl for chlorine, Ag for silver, Na for sodium) absorbs or fluoresces light at a different rate. Each element is instantly recognizable. Uniquely, if cadmium is hit with light, it emits what is called the cadmium redline. That is the basis for the atomic clock."

In four words, "Let there be light," God laid a foundation for time and space, Howard explained. I sat open-mouthed as he continued. "Any farmer knows that the food chain is based on photosynthesis. Without light, you have no vegetation. Without vegetation you can't have animals or humans."

He talked about color. Without light there is no color. There is no rainbow. No spectacular Hawaiian sunsets. No aurora borealis. When the lights are out at the Louvre in Paris, you won't see Mona Lisa's smile.

That car ride literally changed how I saw God, the universe, Scripture, time, art, and Interstate 80. Actually, it changed how I saw lunch. Hanging out with Howard wasn't just about chemistry. It was about seeing the joy of the Creator play out in Howard's life as he let his growing faith inform his work.

I have pretty much always been curious, and I have always had great friends. So when I started seeing my friends as teachers, learning really became fun. When I discovered what they did and how they thought, I always walked away enriched. When I was in my twenties, Howard Malmstadt became a metaphor for that process. Almost thirty years later, when I met Mark, it had a similar feel.

I found Mark's focus stimulating. In that first year we met, he told me he wanted to write. That he felt like he *should* write. At first I thought, "Yeah, sure. Lots of folks say that." But then his single-mindedness showed up. He was absolutely determined to put pen to paper, or in his case, fingers to keyboard. When he says now, "I write out of obedience," I believe him. I experienced his laser-like single-mindedness and learned from it big-time. That's precisely what I had seen in Howard.

As Howard grew in his faith, his impact grew. In the 1980s, at a scientific symposium in his honor at the Americana Hotel in New York City, he told his audience, "I have spent most of my career discovering God's creations, but a few years ago I discovered God. All that I am or ever hope to be I owe to Him through His Son, Jesus of Nazareth." That staid crowd of scientists did what they would never ordinarily do. They came to their feet in a standing ovation.

On July 7, 2003, while on a visit to Kona, Hawaii, to do what he loved—teach—Howard died in his sleep. The United States Navy had taken him to Hawaii and beyond in World War II, so it seems right that his body lies alongside his wife, Carolyn Gay, in the United States Military Cemetery near Kona Airport overlooking the Pacific. As light plays off blue ocean and green palms and the sun sinks into the sea, I see it as nature's salute to a man who loved light.

Engage people and life ramps up. I can learn from anyone: a ninety-three-year-old or a three-year-old, a street sweeper or a scientist. When I make a friend, I get smarter. When I make a friend, I get richer. Howard Malmstadt wrote many books. But the book he wrote with his life was the real book to read. That was a page-turner. I couldn't put it down.

When Howard slipped into the back row that spring Sunday morning because he wanted to discover more about God, he met me. I went to Howard's lab because I wanted to learn more about Howard, and I met God. I got the better deal.

Mark's Story

Ralph Waldo Emerson once said, "Every man is my superior in some way. In that, I learn of him."[1] I first discovered that quote in one of my favorite books: *How to Win Friends and Influence People* by Dale Carnegie, and I've tried to live by that maxim ever since. I believe that I have something to learn from everyone. I never have a conversation with someone without having a journal with me because I always write down thoughts and observations. We are all subconsciously programmed and wired by the influencers in our lives. This includes family, friends, teachers, pastors, and coaches. But sometimes there are certain people we invite intentionally into our lives because we think, "I want that person to affect the way I think, the way I make decisions, the way I live." Dick is one of those select few in my life. Actually, when he professed his love of light, I knew we were a mentoring match made in heaven. Just as a certain osmosis took place between Howard Malmstadt and Dick Foth, that same kind of osmosis has happened between Foth and I. So while I've never met Howard Malmstadt, he's had a profound impact on my life through Dick

Foth. And that's the beauty of mentoring and fathering and friending.

Before meeting Dick, I was rather bookish. Dick taught me to read people the way I read books. I discovered, as Dick likes to say, that people are books with skin on them. Their lives are stories to be read and learned from. So while my inclination is more toward book learning than people learning, my relationship with Dick has helped counterbalance that. He has modeled how relationships enrich your life. I have read his biography, not on paper but in person. Of course, this book was my attempt to get it on paper too! I have read the way Foth interacts with people, the way he remembers things, the way he handles situations. I've read Dick for nearly two decades now, and in my mind, he's a bestseller.

If you asked me what human books have made the greatest influence on my life, I'd give you three titles: Dick Foth, Bob Schmidgall, and Bob Rhoden are on my top shelf. I have found that if you can overcome your insecurity and get around people who are much smarter than you are, you can glean from them. When you surround yourself with people you admire, who live life in a way that inspires you, they start to rub off on you. I call it "bumping into someone's anointing." It's not something that can simply be taught. It has to be *caught*.

One of the more meaningful weeks of my life was spent with Jack Hayford at his School of Pastoral Nurture. Jack literally invited us into his life. We spent a week in his classroom and had dinner at his home. That experience helped me understand why Jesus didn't just say to the disciples, "Listen to me." He said, "Follow me." Real learning takes place when you are doing life together. You rub shoulders and share ideas. You inspire and encourage each other. The Scripture that says, "Two are better than one,"[2] takes on new meaning when it comes to learning. I think genius tends to run in packs. Throughout history some of the greatest friendships have changed the world as we know it. J. R. R. Tolkien and C. S. Lewis encouraged each other in a weekly writers' group at Magdalene College at Oxford University. Their friendship spawned some of the greatest mythological literature of our century, The Lord of the Rings and The Chronicles of Narnia. Dr. Henrietta Mears organized the largest Sunday school of her time at First Presbyterian Hollywood with 6,500 in attendance. She developed the curriculum herself. But her development didn't stop with curriculum. She developed people. Those she touched with her humor, her excitement for God, and her love for Scripture included Billy Graham, Young Life founder Jim Rayburn, Navigators founder Dawson Trotman, United States Senate Chaplain Richard Halverson, and Campus Crusade for Christ founder Bill Bright. That is one amazing Sunday school class! That is the kind of reach and influence that will be felt for centuries to come.

If I had to reduce my life mission into a single sentence, it would be this: helping others maximize their God-given potential. Potential is God's gift to you. What you do with it is your gift back to God. My greatest joy as a pastor and parent and friend is seeing someone in their sweet spot. There is nothing like seeing someone use the God-given gifts that you saw in them before they saw them in themselves. I just stand back and smile.

I have as many insecurities as the next person. Early on, when we had guest preachers in our pulpit, I wanted them to do well but not too well. Now I freely and gladly admit that I'm not even the most gifted teacher or leader on our team. I am the lead pastor, and with that comes a certain gravitas because I've been around the longest, but I can genuinely celebrate the unique gifts each member of our team brings to the table. Harry Truman once said, "It is amazing what you can accomplish if you don't care who gets the credit."[3]

Have you ever met someone who is trying their hardest to impress you? It's unimpressive isn't it? You know what's impressive? Someone who isn't trying to impress at all. If you want to get people interested in you, don't try to be interesting. Show interest in them. No one does this better than Dick Foth. He knows more facts about more people than anyone I know. I honestly don't think there is a person on the planet who is more interested in people than Dick. And isn't that one of the qualities that made Jesus so magnetic? He had an eternal interest in every person He met.

The Greatest Freedom Is Having Nothing to Prove

15

Learn as If You'll Live Forever

 Dick's Story

It was quite a year, 1959. Fidel Castro took power in Cuba. Alaska and Hawaii became the forty-ninth and fiftieth states. Elvis was in the army in Germany. And I enrolled as a seventeen-year-old pre-med student at Cal Berkeley.

I would be forever *pre*-med because Chemistry 1A was my nemesis. I would start toward the chem lab on my trusty Vespa, and suddenly I was ten miles away in the east Oakland Hills, pulling into Paul and Vi Pipkin's driveway.

Going to the Pipkins' was fun because they had delicious food, cute daughters, and great stories about Asia. The best part of their house was the garage. It had no cars, just books. At the heart of those stolen hours was *China's Millions*. Paul had scores of that periodical published by turn-of-the-century missionary Hudson Taylor.

In a dim garage with scents of motor oil and new carpet, I would feel the adventures and suffering and miracles. One moment I was tacking up the Yangtze River on a rickety sampan. The next I was slurping a bowl of green tea with the cracked shells of sunflower seeds dribbling off my chin, in the custom of the day. Grueling walks, steaming tea, sunflower seeds, and Jesus. I was all over it.

I was getting a D in Chemistry and an A in China. It wasn't long before Cal and I quit each other. My Vespa found its way seventy-five miles south to the Santa Cruz Mountains so I could start my sophomore year at Bethany College. It was there I began to dream of being a missionary in far-off lands, possibly even China.

Ology means "a branch of knowledge." How we get that knowledge is the fun part. Books have only been around for the last seven hundred years. Before that, it was some handwritten parchments and a lot of storytellers. Oral tradition was really the name of the game. Everyone spoke, but hardly anyone read. When reading kicked in, the world contracted and expanded at the same time. People could go places without going places. And they could do it again and again.

Learning from others happens two ways: firsthand or secondhand. For a firsthand account, you talk to people. For a secondhand account, you read books about them. Biographies are my favorite.

Without question, for me, the world's greatest biography is that of Jesus of Nazareth. Many have written of this thirty-three-year-old Jewish carpenter executed by the state two thousand years ago. The United States Library of Congress, with more than thirty-six million volumes, has more books about this Jesus than any other person. Lincoln and Napoleon, to my understanding, are a distant second. If you have to choose one biography, choose His. It was written by four men—Matthew, Mark, Luke, and John. If you read the story seriously, it's a game changer. When you read what He says and see what He does, the evidence is stark: *He is way more than a religious figure.*

Millions believe that Jesus Christ of Nazareth is God. Even if you don't, His story intrigues and His ideas disturb. I'll never forget a conversation I overheard. An Oxford-educated ambassador from a very different religious background from mine was asked, "Mr. Ambassador, have you been thinking much about Jesus lately?" He said, "You know, I have. I began reading the Gospels, and Jesus is a very interesting man!" You can say that again. The ambassador was starting exactly where Jesus starts in the story, as the Son of Man. To know him as God comes by revelation.

To be able to *know* anything is a gift from God. To find that knowledge by reading is a grand adventure. When we read about someone doing the impossible, we start to believe the impossible is possible. When we read of passion and triumph and failure, we see that no one is perfect. We need to know that imperfect people can lead imperfect lives and still impact the world around them in powerful ways. That lets us in.

David Livingstone is a name linked with sacrifice, exploration, and adventure in Africa in the mid-1800s. He was a tough Scot with monumental reach as an explorer, abolitionist, scientist, champion of trade, and proponent of Christian missions in central Africa. When he died in present-day Zambia, as a gesture of love, his friends cut his heart out and buried it in a tin box under a mvula tree in Chief Chitambo's village. His body was then carried a thousand miles to the coast and sent back to England, where it lies today in Westminster Abbey. But all was not perfect.

Livingstone's body lies in London. His son Robert's body lies 3,800 miles away in a mass grave near Salisbury, North Carolina. Apart from his father for many years, he was raised by two aunts in Scotland. When his mother died, Robert was determined to find his father in Africa. Without permission, he sailed for Durban, South Africa. When he arrived, his father had already left on his Zambezi River expedition. The letter he left for Robert forbid him to come further. History does not tell us why. Disheartened, Robert sailed to America and enlisted in a New Hampshire Regiment at the height of the Civil War under the name Rupert Vincent. He was wounded and died in a Confederate POW camp in Salisbury on December 5, 1864. His father would die of malaria in Africa nine years later.

No great leader is perfect. But we can still be inspired by the model of Livingstone's triumphs and learn from his mistakes as we live out our own adventures. We can learn from any genre, from theology to allegory to poetry to fiction. When I read biography, I love good heroes. Louis L'Amour, the iconic Western writer, has great heroes and wisdom. Some of his ideas paraphrased would sound like this: Know that when trouble hits, family will come a-runnin'. Don't undervalue the love and partnership of a good woman. Always know where the exits are in the room. Always know where the nearest watering hole is.

L'Amour was an adventurer and a reader himself. His characters often carry a couple of books in their saddlebags. Books allow us to know each other's stories when we aren't sitting around the same campfire.

Coming back to Jesus of Nazareth and the Gospels, I want to close my reflection here with this thought. John concludes his Gospel by saying that the world could not contain all the books that could be written about what Jesus did. Book upon book upon book upon book. Consider this one more of those. His life is the best model. His sacrifice saves my whole life. His methods are opposite of ours. The dreams that He inspires change the world. The adventure He calls us to is the one that counts. The move He made transforms life forever.

When you read the book, you learn about Him secondhand. When you meet Him firsthand? That is *real knowledge*.

Mark's Story

In the tenth century, Abdul Kassem Ismael, the Grand Vizier of Persia, was a man devoted to his books. He took book learning and book loving to a new level. He was a scholar who traveled far and wide curating for his collection. His library, which consisted of 117,000 volumes, was a sight to behold—mostly because it was a mobile library. He strapped his library to the backs of four hundred camels and trained them to walk in alphabetical order. The Dewey decimal system pales by comparison! Each camel driver became a well-trained librarian, able to find the book the Grand Vizier required at a moment's notice. This scholar took cultivating his mind seriously. I like his style.

The human brain weighs three pounds. It is the size of a softball, and yet with it we have the capacity to learn something new every second of every minute of every hour of every day for the next three hundred million years. God has created us with an unlimited capacity to learn. What that tells me is that we ought to keep learning until the day we die.

Leonardo da Vinci once observed that the average human "looks without seeing, listens without hearing, touches without feeling, eats without tasting, inhales without awareness of odor or fragrance, and talks without thinking."[1] But not da Vinci. The quintessential Renaissance man called the five senses *the ministers of the soul*. Perhaps no one in history stewarded them better than he did. Famous for his paintings *The Last Supper*, *Mona Lisa*, and *Vitruvian Man*, da Vinci was a first-class noticer. Da Vinci never went anywhere without his notebooks, in which he recorded ideas and observations in mirror-image cursive. His journals contain the genesis of some of his most ingenious ideas—a helicopter-like contraption he called an orinthopter, a diving suit, and a robotic knight. But the thing that amazes me most is that while on his own deathbed, he meticulously noted his own symptoms in his journal. That's devotion to learning. Seven thousand pages of da Vinci's journals have been preserved. And in case you care, Bill Gates purchased eighteen pages for $30.8 million a few decades ago.

I never go anywhere without my journal. Next to my Bible, it's most sacred. It doesn't matter where I'm praying, listening to a message, or meeting with someone, I'm always writing in my journal. It's the way I take thoughts captive and make them obedient to Christ.[2]

The word *disciple* in the Greek literally means *learner*. So by definition, a disciple is someone who never stops learning. The pivot point in my life was a basketball road trip when I was twenty years old. I read an eight-hundred-page biography of Albert Einstein. Somewhere on Interstate 44 between Kansas City and Springfield, Missouri, I fell in love with books. I read nearly two hundred books that year, and I read at that pace for nearly a decade. Einstein said one thing in that biography that has become a personal mantra of mine: "Never lose a holy curiosity."[3] To piggyback on Dick's philosophy of learning, I would suggest that *every ology is a branch of theology*. Each new thing we learn shouts to us of the creativity and greatness of our God, whether it is biology, zoology, psychology, or archeology.

Einstein famously observed, "Science without religion is lame, religion without science is blind."[4] I've found that a little knowledge of science adds dimensionality to my theology. The man born blind is a good example. The Bible specifically says that no one had ever heard of a man born blind being healed. Here's why: someone born blind would have had no synaptic pathway between the optic nerve and visual cortex in the brain. This is not an astigmatism or cataract. This is nothing short of synaptogenesis—the creation of new synapses. A little knowledge of neurology goes a long way in fully appreciating this unprecedented miracle.

I read once that it takes the average author about two years of writing and researching to write a book. So I figured I was getting two years of life experience with every book I read. And life experience is exactly what I lacked when I was a twenty-six-year-old lead pastor. My first year of pastoring, I read about two hundred books. Hey, there were only twenty-five people attending NCC at the time. I had some time on my hands! I gained four hundred years of life experience in a 365-day period. I've only taken forty-four trips around the sun, but in book years, I'm at least six thousand years old.

As Oliver Wendell Holmes once said, when a person's mind is stretched by a new idea, it never returns to its original dimensions.[5] So when I read a book, my mind takes on a new shape. I've read with great intentionality, in particular, about subjects I know very little about. It's the way I cross-pollinate my mind. And it's one key to creativity. When you juxtapose ideas from different realms of knowledge, you often have an *aha moment*. I like learning from different disciplines, then bringing that knowledge to bear in the field to which God has called me. One good book, one good idea can totally alter your outlook on life.

When National Community Church was five years old, we had a couple hundred people, not a lot of money, and one church with one location. I really felt like God was calling us to go multisite. I had a vision, at the corner of 5th and F Street NE, of a Metro map. I could see NCC meeting in movie theaters near Metro stops all over the DC area. I didn't know how we would get there or what that would look like. There wasn't even a word to describe what I envisioned. *Multisite* wasn't in the ecclesiological dictionary at that point. But we researched, planned, and prepared, and then I finally cast the vision to the church to go multisite. The thing that gave me the freedom to do so was one statement in Andy Stanley's *Next Generation Leader*. He said, "You are probably never going to be more than about 80 percent certain."[6] Up until that point, I had operated with a mentality that I needed to be 99 percent certain. But if you only act when you are 99 percent certain, you are not going to do much of anything. That one sentence set me free and became a part of my paradigm. One footnote: if we're talking about marriage, I'd shoot for more than 80 percent certainty! But for most everything else, I'd set the bar right about there.

As a perfectionist, I have made Ecclesiastes 11 a prescription of sorts. I want a money-back guarantee of success, but I've learned that sometimes you have to "cast your bread upon the waters."[7] In other words, don't wait until you are ready. If you do, you'll be waiting for the rest of your life! I don't think I've been ready to do anything God has called me to. I'm not saying I wasn't prepared. I was. But I've learned to live by this sequence: "Go. Set. Ready."

Ecclesiastes 11:6 says, "Sow your seed in the morning, and at evening let your hands not be idle, for you do not know which will succeed, whether this or that, or whether both will do equally well." If you wait for the right cloud formation or until the planting conditions are perfect, you will never do anything. All you need is a green light from God. Then throw caution to the wind and go for it.

One of my linchpin verses is 1 Corinthians 8:2: "If anyone thinks that he knows anything, he knows nothing yet as he ought to know" (NKJV). True knowledge should not produce pride; it should produce humility. Why? Because the more you know, the more you know how much you don't know. Knowledge in the realm of natural revelation gives more dimensionality to special revelation. Simply put, a little understanding of chemistry enhances our appreciation of Jesus' mutating water molecules and turning them into wine. A little understanding of agriculture gives new depth to Jesus' parables of the sower and the seed. More knowledge equals more potential for worship.

The astronomer who charts the stars or the geneticist who maps the genome or the chemist who synthesizes compounds to make pharmaceuticals is studying the Creator by researching His creation. I believe that the more we learn, the more we honor Him, because we're stewarding the three pounds of gray matter He has given us. We should be students of life, discovering new things each and every day on earth. And then we can spend the next thousand years studying Him!

Many years ago, I got a coffee mug from Amazon.com with a Mahatma Gandhi quote imprinted on it. I no longer use the mug, but I've never forgotten the quote: "Live as if you'll die tomorrow. Learn as if you'll live forever." That last line has become a motto of mine. It's no coincidence that my top strength on the StrengthsFinder assessment is *learner*. If I'm not learning, I'm not happy. And while that may not be your particular strength, the word *disciple* literally means *learner*. So one way or the other, there is no escaping it. Learning is the heart of discipleship. You can't just take up your cross daily. You need to take up the Bible every day. And I'd recommend at least a chapter a day from your book of choice.

The French writer Jacques Réda had a peculiar habit—he used to walk the streets of Paris with the intention of seeing one new thing each day. It was the way he renewed his love for the city. I think we renew our love for the Creator the same way. Our love grows deeper as we discover new dimensions of His character through His creation.

Never Lose a Holy Curiosity

16

Success Is Succession

> **Dick's Story**

Old people I talk to know a few things. They used to know more. Circling the sun tends to burn off the certainties of the young.

I first heard the phrase "a trip around the sun" from my psychologist friend Dick Dobbins. He spoke of the aging process as "taking a trip around the sun with atmospheric pressure at fourteen pounds per square inch every mile of the way." Then he paused and said, "You do that sixty or seventy times and you get weaker and slower and stuff starts moving around!" Having traveled seventy-two times around the sun, that's a bit close to home. There is one thing, however, that gets stronger with age: *perspective*.

I heard Dr. J. Edwin Orr, a renowned church historian with doctorates from both Northwestern University and Oxford, relate an intriguing anecdote some years ago. As a chaplain on the Pacific island of Moratai in World War II, he was cornered by a young soldier who, having witnessed carnage beyond belief, said, "I am an atheist. There is no God!" Musing on that challenge, Orr said, "Son, how much of all there is to know do you think you know?" Taken aback, the young man faltered. Dr. Orr continued, "Let's give you the benefit of the doubt and be exceedingly generous. Let's say you know one quarter of one percent of all there is to know in the entire universe. Do you think that perhaps somewhere in that other ninety-nine and three-quarters percent there just might be a God?" The next day the young fellow returned and said, "Okay. I'm not an atheist. I'm an agnostic. There might be a god, but I can't know him." Wisdom takes time.

Wisdom rides on the heels of those who have spent lots of years circling the sun. If it were just the accumulation of knowledge, we all would be wise. We live in a day that has more information than we could use in three thousand lifetimes. More new knowledge has been created this year than in the past five thousand years combined. The result: we are overwhelmed with information and dying for wisdom.

Wisdom shows up in delightful places. I met Charles Daniels on the tail end of a storm. Ruth and I had taken our kids to the Outer Banks of North Carolina in June of 1972. Hurricane Agnes had just paid a visit. Sitting on Cape Hatteras pier with the abating hurricane's winds still blowing like mad, I watched a forty-something man, deeply tanned, with pale blue eyes and khakis rolled up to his knees, stroll toward me.

I said, "How are you doing?"

He said, "Fine." It sounded like *foyne*. His accent was a delightful cross between the east end of London and Andy Griffith.

Introducing myself, I asked, "Are you a fisherman?"

He said, "Yes, but I ain't goin' out today. It's blowin' too hard." Then he asked, "What do you do?"

"I'm a pastor," I said.

"I ain't no preacher," he replied, "but I've been saved fifteen years and proud of it!"

Wind snatching words away, he said, "What're you doin' in the mornin'?"

I said, "Nothing."

He said, "Do you wanna go fishin' wi' me?" Done deal. At 5:00 the next day, the *Miss Molly* chugged out into Pamlico Sound, that body of water no deeper than twenty feet separating the mainland from the Outer Banks. It runs for a hundred miles down the Atlantic seaboard and is eighteen miles at its widest point. Some of the richest fishing in the world is found there with three saltwater inlets from the sea and five freshwater rivers from the piedmont of Carolina.

I ate grits for the first time in my life on that boat, which Charles had built with his own hands. He stretched a mile of nets between two boats and proceeded to drag the sound for four hours, then bunt up the nets. By circling these two boats around, the fishermen made the net encompass a space about ten or fifteen feet in diameter. Then they drove stakes into the floor of the sound to hold the net in place and trap the fish. It was exhilarating. It was exciting. It was the beginning of a friendship that has spanned decades.

Charles is a fount of good-natured, earthy wisdom grounded in Scripture and common sense. Years after our first meeting in Cape Hatteras, on that crazy trip to Catalina Island with some other friends, we talked about life and family and work. We had an hour-long discussion about how people come in the front door of church and slip out the back door without ever being truly engaged. We argued about the best ways to help guys grow spiritually. Finally, somebody said, "Charles, what are your thoughts?" He said, "Well, it sounds to me like you fellers ain't settin' your nets tight enough! You need to stake the nets down so them fish can't scoot out under it." Now, that's called wisdom.

Wisdom is the distillation of experience. If we invite God into our experience, it becomes concentrated and focused in a way that is true and easy to understand. Proverbs 3:5–6 says, "Trust in the LORD with all your heart, and do not lean on your own understanding. In all your ways acknowledge him, and he will make straight your paths" (ESV). It is the process of years yielded to God, to His understanding, to His ways, that births wisdom.

We need to enjoy the accumulation of years under our belt. A friend near Chicago has a sign hanging in her kitchen that says, "Some people want to turn back the clock. Not me. I want people to know why I look this way. I've traveled a lot of roads in my life and not all of them were paved."

I may not be getting younger, but hopefully I am becoming more real. It reminds me of the exchange in *The Velveteen Rabbit* between the old Skin Horse and the Rabbit when they are lying side by side on the nursery floor.

> "What is REAL?" asked the Rabbit one day, when they were lying side by side near the nursery fender, before Nana came to tidy the room. "Does it mean having things that buzz inside you and a stick-out handle?"
>
> "Real isn't how you are made," said the Skin Horse. "It's a thing that happens to you. When a child loves you for a long, long time. . . . That's why it doesn't happen often to people who break easily, or have sharp edges, or who have to be carefully kept. Generally, by the time you are Real, most of your hair has been loved off, and your eyes drop out and you get loose in the joints and very shabby."[1]

I think in a culture where age is something to be staved off or feared, we miss out on the experience of becoming wise. We miss out on the now. We need to let life make us real. The truth is that with each year I get to know a little more about life, a little more about myself and the people I love, and a little more about God. Jesus the Eternal One, more than any other person, helps me embrace the now. What a gift that is!

If you can see your trips around the sun in terms of enrichment and ongoing renewal, of deeper exploration and broader reach, wrinkles translate to richness. Mark is wise beyond his years. Perhaps it's because he actually reflects and muses as he circles the sun. You wouldn't think an action-oriented guy would do that so much. But he does. And we get the product: wisdom.

Tom Paterson is a genius in organizational management, having worked in corporate planning with Douglas Aircraft, IBM, and RCA, among others. At this writing, Tom has circled the sun more than eighty-nine times and spent most of his working life thinking strategically. Along the way, he has reflected on a strategic plan for life itself. And though he has suffered greatly through the years with the deaths of spouses and children, he has not become embittered. Quite the opposite. He is a gentle and kindly soul with a depth you can feel as you sit with him. If you ask him the essence of his plan? He simply says, "Surrender. Surrender to Jesus and everything flows."

That, it seems to me, is the wisest truth of all.

Mark's Story

A few years ago, our family moved to a new house on Capitol Hill, half a block from our old house. I think we set a U-Haul record for the least mileage on a moving van. It cost $0.47 in mileage charges, but that didn't make the move any easier, of course, because we still had to pack and unpack everything we had accumulated during the fourteen years we lived in our first house. During the process of unpacking, I came across an old box that I had not seen in many years. I stopped my frenzied work and took a leisurely stroll down memory lane. The next hour felt like a lifetime because that box contained a lifetime of memories.

The contents were both worthless and priceless: a Kong Phooey lunchbox that doubled as a sacrosanct container for my vintage football cards, a gold medal from the Awana Olympics, a fourth-grade art project that somehow made the keepsake cut, the flat shoe I wore while recovering from a broken ankle in high school, and an occupational assessment I took in grad school which showed a below average aptitude for writing.

As I rummaged through old journals and photo albums, I realized that part of me was still in that box. It reminded me of one of my favorite books, *Tuesdays with Morrie*, which is one of the inspirations for this book. The author, Mitch Albom, interviews his old college professor, Morrie Schwartz, who shares reflections on life as he fights Lou Gehrig's disease to the death. The book is full of profundities, but the most memorable for me is an exchange about aging. Morrie says to Mitch, "I *embrace* aging. . . . It's very simple. As you grow, you learn more. If you stayed at twenty-two, you'd always be as ignorant as you were at twenty-two." Then Morrie shares a perspective on life that ought to be internalized sooner rather than later or younger rather than older. "The truth is, part of me is every age. I'm a three-year-old, I'm a five-year-old, I'm a thirty-seven-year-old, I'm a fifty-year-old. I've been through all of them, and I know what it's like. I delight in being a child when it's appropriate to be a child. I delight in being a wise old man when it's appropriate to be a wise old man. Think of all I can be! I am every age, up to my own."[2]

Dick Foth is my Morrie Schwartz.

The way Dick lives his life has somehow helped me conquer my fear of aging. In fact, more than conquer it—I celebrate it. To be honest, I didn't want to turn forty. But Foth has taught me that age is more than a state of body; it's a state of mind, a state of spirit. And the true beauty of aging is the cumulative wisdom gained, and with it, a profound appreciation for the faithfulness of God. That is precisely why I love aging—the faithfulness of God becomes crystal clear. You connect more dots. At least three times this year, I wanted to scream, "God is faithful!" at the top of my lungs. Once was on a visit to Central Bible College where I'd been a student in the early nineties. The second was during a two-day life planning process in which we mapped my storyline. The third was during our annual planning retreat in which I reviewed strategic plans from the past decade and marveled at what God has done in spite of us!

Back to my shoebox.

I thought of that statement "I am every age, up to my own" as I rummaged through it. The spiritual mementos inside my shoebox don't just reveal who I was. They reveal who I am. The oxygen mask from my stint in the ICU is not just a distant memory; it's part of my daily consciousness. In a sense, I am that shoebox and that shoebox is me. I am more than my name, more than my occupation, more than my degrees, more than my dreams, more than my family. I am who I was. It's my footprints—where I've been and what I've done—that reveal my soulprint. It's my unique combination of memories that makes me who I am spiritually, emotionally, relationally, and motivationally. It's also that unique combination of memories that enables me to worship God in a way that no one else can. Why? Because when a congregation sings the classic hymn "Great Is Thy Faithfulness," it's more than generic praise for a static character trait. God's faithfulness is as unique as every moment of your life! Every memory is a testament to His dynamic faithfulness that is simultaneously the same and different for anyone and everyone else.

I thank God for memory. Without it, we'd have to relearn everything, every day. It's our ability to remember the past that enables us to imagine the future. And that's the point of remembering His faithfulness, isn't it? It fuels our future tense faith.

In my book, success is *succession*.

It's the passing of the baton between the prophets Elijah and Elisha.

It's the wisdom transfer between Morrie Schwartz and Mitch Albom, Dick Foth and Mark Batterson.

If your influence ends with you, it wasn't worth your time and effort. Your life is a dead end. But if you influence the next generation, you won't just enter eternity when you die. *You will live on in the lives of those you leave behind.* That's what spiritual fathering and mothering is all about—leaving a legacy of wisdom that is inherited by the next generation. That's what Dick has done for me.

If Dick had been born in Babylon two thousand years ago, I have a hunch he would have been one of the wise men. He's also the most amazing storyteller I've ever met. It was Dick who taught me that my story is really God's story; my history is *His-story* with a hyphen in it. Every life is a unique translation of Scripture—the Dick Foth version, the Mark Batterson version, and your version. God is writing His story through our lives.

I love the gospel according to Dick Foth. It's one of the most authentic translations I've ever read. And just as Dick stewarded his stories to me, I knew I needed to steward his stories to the world. When Dick was just shy of his seventieth trip around the sun, we hiked up Horsetooth Mountain in Fort Collins, Colorado. There is something about a change in elevation that results in a change of perspective. It helps you see farther in every direction. As we neared the summit, Dick and I made a defining decision to write this book. I honestly can't remember if it was Dick's idea or my idea. But it would prove to be our latest and greatest adventure. My motivation was simple: I didn't want Dick's library of life experiences to go to the grave with him. I hope Dick makes a hundred trips around the sun, but

I jokingly told him we'd better hurry up and write this book before he kicks the can!

Can I share a personal conviction? I honestly believe that everybody has a book in them. I'm not talking about a sci-fi novel or nonfiction how-to. But you have an autobiography in you. I know you do. And you owe it to the next generation to write your autobiography in some form or fashion. It doesn't matter how long or short it is; you've got to pass along the hard-earned lessons life has taught you.

I recently had an hour-long conversation with Paul Young, author of the worldwide best seller *The Shack*. We were on a ferry, on our way to visit our mutual friend, Bob Goff. I'm not sure how it came up in conversation, but Paul said that he wrote *The Shack* for his family. He actually went to Kinkos and had fifteen copies made. Mission accomplished. He never expected the book to sell over twenty million copies. That was neither his mission nor his motivation. He wrote it for his family!

I love that. And I resonate with that. When people ask me who my target audience is as an author, I tell them that it's my great-grandchildren. I usually get a confused look, which I try to further confound. I tell them that I know next to nothing about my great-grandfather. Only one story, in fact. He worked as a train conductor, and when they chugged down the tracks near his home, he'd blow the whistle so my grandmother knew it was time to get dinner ready. That's it. That's the sum total of my knowledge about my great-grandfather. I'm not even sure what his last name was. I want my great-grandchildren to know what I thought, what I believed, what I valued. And that's why I write. Books are time capsules that I send to the third and fourth generation. I may never meet them, but they will meet me in the pages of the books I write.

I used to think of learning as something that happened in the context of a classroom. I learned from lectures given by professors with lots of letters behind their names. It wasn't until I met Dick Foth that I realized that learning happens best in the context of friendship and mentorship. Life is the lecture hall. And the curriculum is any and every situation you find yourself in. I simply needed someone who had been there and done that.

It would be impossible for me to put a price tag on the wisdom Dick has shared with me, but it's definitely worth more than all of my graduate degrees combined. I've borrowed more than I could possibly pay back! But there is a way for me to pay it off—by loaning my wisdom to the next generation.

The More You Know, the More You Know How Much You Don't Know

17

Reverse Mentoring

Pagan gods, the Easter bunny, and Jesus. That's where it began. Kids love celebrations, and my wife, Ruth, is the celebratory queen! Not just the Big Three: birthdays, graduations, and Christmas. Getting a B+ in reading, the first day of school, the twenty-third day of school, lost teeth, found artwork, surviving the dentist, and growing a half-inch all qualify. Each moment is worthy of an ice cream cone or chocolate in any form.

One spring early in our marriage, I walked into the house to find Ruth busy in the kitchen with the kids. I asked what was up. She said, "Just coloring these eggs so we can hide them in the yard." I said, "Can't do that. It's an ancient Egyptian fertility rite." She said, "I don't know about that. We're just putting color on these eggs." I said, "No, it is an ancient Egyptian cultic thing."

She looked at me with what I think was pity and said, "My grandparents and parents both did this with us. Are you telling me they are pagan?" I quickly said, "No! No!" Not good to go the pagan route with in-laws.

Then, with a glint in her eye and a hint of a smile, she said, "Our kids know the difference between Jesus and the Easter bunny."

Well, of course they did.

Before that, we had gone to grad school in Illinois as newly-weds without much knowledge of marriage or children. Some friends of ours had two boys, ages four and two. One night, we babysat and it came time for bed. After telling the four-year-old a very cool story like David and Goliath, I said to him, "Okay, let's say our prayers."

He said, "No."

I said, "It's really a good thing to do. It's important."

He replied, "I don't want to."

I was twenty-four. He was four. I tried reason. "Well, God likes us to talk to Him. I think He might be lonely."

At that point this child, who had been on the planet all of fifty-two months, gave me a condescending look and said, "Oh no, Jesus is up there with Him."

Well, of course He was. That boy is now a vascular surgeon in Utah.

I delight in kid wisdom, like the quote from the seven-year-old who says, "I have learned that you can't hide broccoli in a glass of milk." Or what about when a first-grade teacher gives the first half of well-known proverbs to her class for them to complete? Here are just some of the results: "Better to be safe than . . . punch a fifth grader." Or "Strike while the . . . bug is close." And, "You can lead a horse to water, but . . . how?" Gotta love it.

Scripture is full of great kids. Moses is a baby sailor in a reed basket on the Nile River. David the shepherd boy takes on a charging bear to protect his flock. Jesus asks brain-twisting questions of learned leaders in the temple when he's twelve. And the boy in the Gospels brings a sack lunch for the day, and Jesus uses the five loaves and two fish to feed a crowd of more than five thousand. My songwriter friend Ken Jones wrote a musical with this young boy belting out, "If you'd have been there, when he borrowed my lunch, you'd have believed him too!"

Well, of course you would.

I came from a family that had some issues. Even though my parents loved Jesus, over the long haul they found loving each other difficult, and that spilled out into our home. My home was a place of tension for me from junior high on. Ruth's family, on the other hand, had five kids, and her parents enjoyed each other. It's not that they were perfect or didn't have their struggles, but for Ruth, family was a very attractive thing. She brought that bedrock of love and stability into our home. She built on it with her steadiness, home-cooked breakfasts, and treasure hunts in the backyard.

Ruth is built for preschoolers, a pied piper for little people. With that gift she continues to show me that the simplicity of association is what kids are all about. They know if they stick around her, they will come away loved with board games on the floor, puzzles on the table, or big round pancakes on the plate. Quite simply, they trust her.

Walking in sweaty and tired from a tennis game one day in Urbana, I saw our second daughter, four-year-old Jenny, standing at the top of the stairs. I said, "Hi, Jenny," and turned to put my racquet down, only to hear her shout, "Catch me, Daddy!" I whirled to see her in the air and then did my best to catch missile girl as she smashed into my chest a second later. Heart racing, I clutched her to me and said with stern fright, "Jenny! Don't do that! I could drop you!" Grinning, she pressed her cheek to my sweaty face and whispered, "No, you wouldn't. You're my daddy!"

Well, of course I am.

Such trust is spectacular. I may have doubted myself, but Jenny didn't doubt me. When they are loved, children love back with a winsome, unrestrained fierceness. It's a thing of beauty, like wonder.

Curious about everything, kids find wonder in the ordinary. Leaving our house one morning in a three-piece suit, I found our third daughter, Susanna, belly-down in the driveway looking at a fuzzy caterpillar. We called them "woolly worms." "Daddy," she said, "look at this!" I got down on my belly too. Being pressed up against the cement eye to eye with a woolly worm is quite a moment. They have spikes and texture and lots of legs. Susanna just assumed that I'd find wonder facedown on the driveway with her.

Well, of course I would.

That insistent wonder and a child's lack of inhibition are cousins. Kids don't have walls. They are unfiltered truth tellers. Our granddaughter Claire, three at the time, once introduced me to her babysitter by saying, "This is my grandpa and he has no hair."

Well, of course I don't.

I believe God looks at children and sees their longing for "with-ness," the natural intuition, the capacity to love without restraint, the innate curiosity, and He sees Himself. The apostle John says it this way: "as many as received him, to them gave he power to become the sons of God, even to them that believe on his name."[1] Why does he say that? Sounds like an oxymoron. Who thinks of kids and power in the same sentence? Jesus, apparently. When you think about power, who is the most authoritative person in the history of mankind? Jesus! And who is the most submissive person in the history of mankind? Jesus! So when Jesus says, "Unless you change and become like little children, you will never enter the kingdom of heaven,"[2] He is saying, "Become like me."

He is connecting Bethlehem (child) to resurrection (power). He invites us to know and explore and wonder and love without restraint. When He puts it that way, how can we not? Do I want that?

Well, of course I do.

Mark's Story

Sir John Kirk, the nineteenth-century British naturalist, once said that if he had his way, there would always be a little child positioned in the heart of London—perhaps in the precincts of Westminster Abbey or St. Paul's Cathedral. He believed that no one should be allowed to contest a seat in Parliament or become a candidate for public office until he had spent a day with that child and passed an examination in the child's novel methods of thought, feeling, and expression. The first time I read that, I thought, *What a fascinating idea!* Then I realized that is exactly what Jesus did. He proverbially positioned a little child at the epicenter of the kingdom of God.

The best stories I have ever told from the pulpit have been about Parker, Summer, and Josiah. I jokingly call our kids our three little illustrations. About five years ago I began paying them $5 each time I used one of their stories in one of my sermons. If it has an element of embarrassment, they get $20. It's a fun little payoff and a way of saying thanks for letting me share a little bit of their life in my messages. In the past few years, I have supplied them with a steady source of illustration income. They have supplied me with a steady source of life lessons. Their take on life, and the way they see the world around them, teaches me something new each day. Theodor Geisel, better known at Dr. Seuss, said, "Adults are obsolete children." I love that. A lot. And it's a relationship with Christ that reverses the effects of aging. It's a second childhood.

After two master's programs, one doctoral program, and thousands of total hours in the classroom, I have to say that the most powerful, life-changing course I have ever taken is Parenting 101. Graduate school didn't teach me a fraction of what becoming a father has. There are so many experiences I have had as a father that have given me a window into the heart of the heavenly Father. There are so many attributes that my kids possess that remind me of the attributes of Jesus. The closest thing to Christlikeness is childlikeness. That means there is an element of holiness in the daily routine of parenting.

Part of our job as parents is to be students of our children. It's not just so that we can love them for who they are. It's not even so that we can disciple them according to their bent.[3] It's more than that. We need to study them in order to be discipled by them. It's called reverse mentoring, and it's something Dick and I have experienced in our relationship.

For the first few years, our relationship was a one-way street. The knowledge flowed in one direction—from teacher to student. But over the years, I've been able to teach Dick a new trick or two. I'm still the primary beneficiary, no doubt about it, and I'll never be able to give back what I have received from Dick. But I think Dick would be the first to say that some of the greatest moments in our relationship have been those moments when the student has become the teacher. And it's a testament to Dick's character that he actually wants to learn from me.

Back to childlikeness.

At some point in high school, most of us develop a second persona. It's a mask to make us feel more comfortable and accepted. Kids don't have a second persona yet. They are fully themselves all the time. I have a theological theory that when sin was introduced into the world in the Garden of Eden, so was self-consciousness. Adam and Eve discovered that they were naked, and they were ashamed. They were aware of themselves, not to mention their sin, in a way that they never had been before. Inhibitions are not a sign of spiritual maturity. They are a sign of our sinful nature.

In the Garden, we not only lost out on constant communion with our Creator, we also lost out on the ability to truly be ourselves. We have to get back in the presence of the Creator for that to happen. We are most fully ourselves when we are in the presence of the Holy Spirit. And we are the most Christlike when we are the most comfortable in our own skin.

When Parker was a little guy, we had company over for dinner and he came running through the family room yelling, "Captain Underpants!" No inhibitions. No regrets. And no pants! Lora and I quickly put his pants on, but we loved that Parker was completely and totally himself, company or no company. Kids are able to navigate life's journey on the truest level. They are able to find joy every day in being exactly who God created them to be. When you are in God's presence, you can do the same. You can live out your days uninhibited, where you are fully yourself and fully in the moment.

Kids are uninhibited. Kids are also inquisitive.

Writer Ralph B. Smith once made an observation that children ask roughly 125 questions per day and adults ask about 6 questions per day, so somewhere between childhood and adulthood, we lose 119 questions per day. A child's innate curiosity about life is instilled in them at birth by the One who longs to be discovered. The more questions they ask, the more they discover about the world around them. The more they discover about the world around them, the more they discover about the One who made them.

One of the greatest lessons I have learned from my kids is good old-fashioned compassion. We are surrounded by a large homeless community in Washington, DC, and it's easy to become indifferent to those who ask for money. One way we counteract this tendency is by making lunches on Saturday nights for our homeless ministry. Our kids certainly have their selfish moments like everyone else, but not long ago we were walking home from a church gathering and Josiah tugged on my sleeve. "Did you see that guy by the garbage can?" he asked. "I feel like we should help him." Honestly, I hadn't even noticed. So we went back, and I got down on the ground so I could be at the guy's eye level. I asked him his name and how we could help him. The same thing has happened on several occasions. Every time, I'm challenged to be more compassionate, like my children.

My kids stretch me, whether it is Parker challenging my fear of heights by paragliding over the Sacred Valley in Peru or Summer challenging me with her love for orphans. The more they reflect the heart of their heavenly Father, the more I want to reflect the heart of the heavenly Father. As I mentor them, they mentor me. Their childlike qualities encourage me to be like Christ. Their passion for life, their ability to be themselves, their love of discovery, and their innate compassion inspire me daily.

One thing is for sure: when I grow up, I want to be just like them.

The Closest Thing to Christlikeness Is Childlikeness

18

Fully Alive

Dick's Story

The summer I finished Wheaton College grad school, Ruth and I went back to California to work with her dad. Father Blake, as I called him, took me under his wing and began to show me life. One day he sent me to the hospital to check on Mrs. Albrecht, an elderly church member. When I came back, I found him painting a wall in the breezeway between the office and the sanctuary. Physical labor was his default position. Clearing my throat, I said, "Father Blake, I just saw Mrs. Albrecht at the hospital. They say she's terminal." Speaking to the wall, he took another long stroke with the paint roller and simply said, "Aren't we all."

Terminal isn't the way we like to think of ourselves. Immortal is what we like. As children, life is everywhere. As teenagers, we are invincible. As young adults, we are on a mission to find our niche in the world. The reality of death is weird. It's way out there. But death has two defining features: given and inevitable. All are born. All die. As far as we know, only Enoch and Elijah made it off the planet a different way. Our odds are not so good.

In fact, when we have circled the sun a few dozen times, we start counting in terms of years left. Death is coming, and if we are willing to face it, we can focus on the adventure of the now.

Once death comes close, life becomes precious. At the age of three I almost died of complications from scarlet fever. My parents were supposed to be boarding a ship for India from New York and instead were wiring friends and family in the middle of the night to pray for Dickie, as they called me. Those prayers were answered.

A year later I was fighting malignant malaria in the hills of south India. After three days in a delirium with 105-degree temperatures, I am told I turned to my mom and said, "Mommy, I'm going home." Laying her head on the bed, she wept, not knowing if I meant my home in the States or my heavenly home. A knock on the door announced a single Anglican lady, who said she felt she was to pray for me. The fever broke that night.

I only vaguely remember those moments. What I remember with great clarity, however, is a late November afternoon in 1958 at Fremont High School in Oakland. I had won the part of John Proctor in Arthur Miller's *The Crucible* my senior year and was working on my lines with a friend. Taking a break, I was demonstrating my knowledge of how hangings were made to look realistic on television. I stepped up on a chair and said, "Let me show you how this is done." Grabbing a half-inch-thick rope hanging from the grid above us, I tied the rope around my chest, then looped it around my collar. I left some length, so that when I stepped off the chair, my feet would still touch the floor. The best-laid plans. When I stepped off the chair, I did touch the floor for a second—until the rope's elasticity jerked me back up about an inch. I felt a sharp pressure around my throat, then nothing.

At this point in the story I'll cut to my friend, now a psychologist in Tennessee, who at our fiftieth high school reunion at Claremont Hotel in Berkeley, California, recalled the incident.

"Do you remember," he asked, "that time on stage when you almost hung yourself?" I answered that I did. "You know," he said, continuing with the story, "I got you down. I was looking at you and your face turned purple. You started to swing like a pendulum, and I thought, 'Boy! Is that realistic!' Then all of a sudden I realized you were unconscious. You were dead weight. I was trying to lift you, and screaming for somebody to help."

The next thing I remember I was coming to and fighting for a breath. That friend saved my life. I am forever in his debt. For the next two weeks I had to explain my rope-burn necklace.

Some brushes with death leave more of a mark than others. Some marks are burned into our necks and others are burned into our souls. Those marks will change the way we look at life, and how we live that life.

When we are touched by the eternal, it gives us the now in a way that nothing else does. C. S. Lewis said, "If you read history you will find that the Christians who did most for the present world were just those who thought most of the next."[1] One of the things about aging that becomes real in a hurry is that the clock is ticking. I am way closer to death now than that near miss when I was three.

Billy lived in a fancy home in Chicago in the 1890s. At a service in Moody Church, when he was eight, he gave what he knew of himself to what he could understand of Jesus. Eight years later, at sixteen, his father sent him on a trip around the world to expose him to other cultures. He came back captured by the poor and the desperate needs of millions. His father was not pleased because he had planned on Billy taking over the family business. Billy Borden was heir to the Borden Dairy Company.

When Billy enrolled in Yale University in 1904, he was already a multimillionaire. During the course of his four years, he became a leader on campus, starting many small groups for prayer and Bible study. By the time he graduated, it's said that 1,000 of the 1,300 students at Yale were a part of those groups.

His dream was to work with the Muslim population of northern China, but he felt a working knowledge of Arabic would be essential. He went to Cairo for that purpose, but there he contracted spinal meningitis. Borden of Yale, as he would come to be known, died at the age of twenty-five. Some believed it a pity that a life with such potential would be cut short. But one of his Yale colleagues, when hearing that statement, simply noted that a life fully surrendered to Jesus Christ could never be cut short. It would always be just right!

When Borden made the decision to give his life to missions, he wrote the phrase "No reserve" in the back of his Bible with the date next to it. Turning down a job offer from Yale, he added the phrase "No retreat." Then shortly before his death, he added one more phrase: "No regret."

No reserve. No retreat. No regret.

That is Borden's legacy.

One of these days, someone is going to tell you, "Foth died." But don't believe them. My body just fell off. The real Foth goes on forever. Still, I believe earthly days can have eternal impact. The apostle Paul says it well: "I press on toward the goal to win the prize for which God has called me heavenward in Christ Jesus"![12] Life is short. Let's make it count.

Let it be said of us, when we are gone, "That was a life lived *just right!*"

Mark's Story

While teaching at the University of Pennsylvania, Tony Campolo turned an ordinary lecture into an unforgettable life lesson for one of the students sitting on the front row. He asked him, "Young man, how long have you lived?" The student said, "Twenty-three years." Tony said, "No, no, no. That is how long your heart has been pumping blood. That is not how long you have lived." Then Tony told a story about his first visit to the Empire State Building in 1944. At the time it was the tallest building in the world. He was only nine years old, but seventy years later it's a unforgettable memory. Nine-year-old Tony ran around the observation deck taking in the view. Then he caught himself and said to himself, "Tony, you are on top of the Empire State Building." In that one magical moment, time stood still. Tony said, "If I were to live a million years, that moment would still be part of my consciousness because of the way in which I lived it. I was fully alive."

Then Tony said to the student in the front row, "Now let me ask you the question again. How long have you lived?" The student looked back at him and said, "Dr. Campolo, when you say it that way, maybe an hour, less than that, maybe a minute, maybe two minutes. Most of my life has been the meaningless passage of time between all too few moments that I was genuinely alive."[3]

Life isn't measured in minutes. It's measured in moments. It's not the length of days that really matters. It's the stewardship of moments. I think that's the sentiment behind the psalmist's exhortation: "Teach us to number our days."[4] In other words, make each day count. Right before his one hundredth birthday, legendary basketball coach John Wooden reflected on his philosophy of life: "Make *each* day your masterpiece. When you do that as the weeks and months and years . . . unfold behind you, you'll have the deepest self-satisfaction knowing your life has really meant something. You will have achieved the most important kind of success, namely, becoming the best that you are capable of becoming."[5]

So how do you number your days?

I think there is a literal dimension to this exhortation. I count my blessings by literally numbering them in my journal, and I try to do the same with my days. It's as simple as multiplying your age by 365, then adding the number of days since your last birthday. The higher the number, the more you appreciate the fact that His mercies are new every morning.[6]

Figuratively speaking, we number our days by keeping our eyes on eternity. We have a common destiny: we will one day stand before the throne of God. So every moment should be lived in light of eternity. The challenge, according to seventeenth-century French philosopher Blaise Pascal, is that "Our imagination so magnifies this present existence, by the power of continual reflection on it, and so attenuates eternity, by not thinking of it at all, that we reduce an eternity to nothingness, and expand a mere nothing to an eternity."[7] In other words, we think so much about the present and so little about eternity that we turn eternity into nothing and nothing into eternity.

Two years ago, Lora and I were having coffee with my brother-in-law, Matt, and Lora's sister, Amanda. A month earlier, out of the blue, Matt had been diagnosed with a congenital heart defect. He had a routine doctor's visit and the next thing you know, they were scheduling him for open-heart surgery. Matt was twenty-nine at the time. He had been told that when he went into the hospital, the surgeon would open up his chest and put a new valve in. There was between a .2 and .4 percent chance that he would die. Amanda had already lost her dad in her teens. She was not ready to lose her husband in her twenties. But when I asked Matt how he was doing, he said, "This is the greatest gift I've ever been given." His life had been radically changed by this prognosis. He said, "Anytime I'm not reading my Bible or praying, I feel like I'm wasting time."

Death puts life into perspective.

One night not long ago, we were driving by Washington Hospital Center in downtown DC. I turned to my oldest son, Parker, and said, "That's where your dad almost died." That was a blunt thing to say, but death is blunt. It's a gut job. It strips everything down to the studs. What matters most is revealed. What is truly important becomes the focus.

When I almost died from ruptured intestines, it wasn't just a medical miracle that transpired in that hospital. It was a soul shift. When I realized I was getting a second chance at living, I was infused with a new sense of gratefulness. It is a lot harder to take life for granted when you realize how quickly it can be snatched away. G. K. Chesterton said that his goal in life was to take nothing for granted—not a sunrise, not a smile, not a flower, nothing. That is a truly wonderful approach to life. Don't take anything for granted. Truly appreciate every minute that you have to live. My near-death experience has helped me be better at that. If I hadn't almost died, I wouldn't have figured out how to live.

When I was in my twenties, I resisted the idea of aging. I wanted to be the young guy forever. But the older I get, the more I appreciate each trip around the sun because I'm accumulating irrefutable evidence of God's goodness, of God's faithfulness. Like Chesterton knew, each sunrise, each sunset, each full moon adds richness to my life. It's not that I'm getting older with each birthday; it's that I am adding more to my life with each passing year. There is something about being friends with someone who is three decades my senior that has eliminated the fear of aging. I actually embrace it because I see the advantages of age. And right at the top of the list is witnessing the faithfulness of God that spans the decades.

I recently returned to my hometown of Naperville, Illinois, with our family. We drove all around town showing the kids the old spots where we used to hang out—the old school, the old church, where I got my first ticket, and where I got my first kiss. With each place we visited, it was like God was screaming, "I'm faithful!" And He screams it louder and louder with each lap around the sun!

Most people celebrate one birthday, but I get to celebrate two. November 5 is my first birthday, but my second birthday is July 23. That is the day I got my second chance at living after spending two days on a respirator, hanging on to life. To be honest, my second birthday is even more meaningful to me than my first birthday. At this writing, I'm fourteen years old. And that's how I feel. Whenever I hit a tough spot, I just go back to July 23 and think, *I've been worse than I am now, and I've gone through tougher times. This may be bad, but I'm still breathing.* When you come face-to-face with death, you are bound and determined to truly live. In fact, I'd love to live to a hundred. I'm probably the least likely candidate given my medical history. But no matter how long I live, I'm going to squeeze as much adventure out of every day as I possibly can.

Martin Luther lived his life with this mandate pulsing through his veins: "Preach [and live] as if Jesus was crucified yesterday, rose from the dead today, and is returning tomorrow." I love the sense of urgency in that sentiment. And it's that kind of urgency that typically accompanies a life well lived. Only God knows your allotted number of days. But it's your job to redeem the time.[8] You don't get to choose the final outcome of your life, but you do get to choose your outlook. Choose gratitude. Choose adventure. Choose risk. Choose life.

Quit living as if the purpose of life is to arrive safely at death. Let today be your second birthday. Tomorrow is not guaranteed, so make today count. Make it your masterpiece.

Live as If Christ Was Crucified Yesterday, Rose from the Dead Today, and Is Returning Tomorrow

19

Lineage and Legacy

➤ Dick's Story

Lineage and legacy are not the same. They may be linked, but they are not synonymous. Lineage is a given. Legacy is a gift. We have two lineage streams in our marriage: Foth/Boyd and Blakeley/Presnell. Gerhard Foth arrived in Michigan from Poland in the 1890s, and the Boyds showed up who-knows-when in the 1800s from Northern Ireland. The Blakeley and Presnell families, on the other hand, lived just a few miles apart in North Carolina in the late 1760s but didn't know each other. As America headed west to California, so did our families.

In 1933 Oliver Foth married Gwen Boyd in southern California. Roy Blakeley married Opal Presnell there in 1938. From that lineage the two legacies that have impacted me most are from Gwen, my mother, and Roy, my father-in-law. She with her grit. He with his grace.

I first met Roy Blakeley when I was ten. We had been home from India three years, and I went to my very first summer kids' camp. Nestled in towering redwoods, the place was rustic with bunks that were okay and food that sure wasn't Mama's. The speaker, though, was something.

Roy showed up dressed in his World War II army fatigues with a .38 revolver on his hip. He was a ventriloquist and had a dummy named Jimmy. Clearly, Roy liked kids. He seemed to think we were actually people.

I sat on the front row at the gathering each night because I liked Jimmy, and I was thrilled when Roy fired his .38. It had blanks, of course, but each time he did it, I nearly jumped out of my skin. He was creative, engaging, affirming, stable, and present. I just loved being around him. Ten years later I loved being around his daughter, Ruth.

On Christmas Eve 1962, with a modest engagement ring firmly ensconced in a small box inside another box inside another box inside a big box, I drove 110 miles from Santa Cruz, California, to the San Joaquin farming town of Modesto. The night air was cold when I called the Blakeley home from a gas station off Highway 99. Startled when Ruth answered, I masked my voice and said, "Could I speak to Pastor Blakeley please?" My heart thumped quick and hard in my chest. "I'll get him," she said.

His signature three-tone "Hello?" was the next thing I heard. I said, "Pastor Blakely, this is Dick. Don't let Ruth know it's me." He said, "Yes sir, I understand." I said, "I need to talk to you. Could you meet me in the parking lot at Stanislaus School?" He said, "Is it an emergency?" "Yes, I have a heart problem." He said, "I'll come immediately!" And he hung up.

Fifteen minutes later Roy wheeled a battered pickup into the school parking lot. A farmer at heart, he sported a sweatshirt, rumpled khakis, and a greasy cap. Clambering into the passenger side I said, "Thanks for coming." "Glad to do it," he said.

Then I blurted, "I just want you to know that I really love your daughter, Ruth." He smiled and said, "We kinda like her too." I said, "I'd like to marry her." He said, "Well, I think that could be arranged." I said, "But I'm scared because, as you know, my parents have struggled in their marriage. I don't think they are going to make it, and I have this fear that maybe it's hereditary or something." He said, "I understand." With great kindness in his eyes, he put his hand on my shoulder and said, "Dick, why don't you love Jesus and Ruthie, and Opal and I will walk with you. It will be okay. I trust you."

Those words upended my world. That expression of trust was the first installment of the legacy I would receive for the next thirty years.

Roy never understood what couldn't be done. He started one of the earliest private evangelical schools in Modesto. He launched Mission to Mexico trips in the 1960s for high schoolers and collegians to work with the poor. He built a senior citizens' retirement center with HUD money. He helped Russian families immigrate to the United States. For their five children and twenty-three grandchildren, he modeled vision and grace. I watched how he did it. Been practicing now for more than fifty years. Not quite there.

When Gwen Boyd married six-foot-two-inch Oliver Foth in 1933, they began a journey that took them to northern California, southern India, western Missouri, and back to California. They were gifted, high-impact people. My sister and I were privileged to be in their home. But over time things unraveled. Four months after I married Ruth in the summer of 1963, we got a letter from my dad saying that he was leaving my mom.

She was fifty-three years old and had never worked outside the home. She was bright and talented, a consummate pianist and organist. Her survival skills from the Great Depression, World War II, and life as an expatriate in South India kicked in. Moving to Southern California near my sister, she taught herself to type. With that skill she was hired at Huntington Memorial

Hospital in Pasadena as an admitting clerk, and she worked there until she was seventy-one. At that point management said, "Gwen, you've been great, but you must stop." Whereupon she went across the street to a rather posh assisted-living facility, got a job, and worked until she was eighty-two. She came from the generation that thrived on duty, responsibility, and "doing what needed to be done."

Her love for Jesus, her family, and her music kept her going. Her humor kept her sane. The Boyds were always laughers, and though she couldn't laugh *at* her circumstances, she laughed *in* them. Even after ninety-five, when dementia began to visit, humor triumphed. On her ninety-sixth birthday, I called her from Washington, DC, saying, "Hi, Mom, this is Dick." In response, she turned to someone and said, "My brother's on the phone!" She had four brothers, none of whom was named Dick. I said, "Mom, this is Dick, your son!" She exclaimed, "Dick, honey! You live way over there, don't you?" I said, "Yes, I live in Washington, DC." She said, "You know, I have a son in Washington, DC." "That's me, Mom!" I said. At which juncture, she chortled, "There must be two of you!" Dementia is not funny, but my mom was funny.

She had great genes, and it took a lot of years for her age to catch up. At ninety-two she was still driving on California freeways. She pretty much drove her age. You may have seen her.

Mom died in August 2010 at one hundred years of age. She was born in 1910, when Taft was president and there were only one thousand miles of paved roads in the entire country. In her century she saw two world wars, the Great Depression, and the advent of cars, air travel, movies, television, credit cards, and Dr. Seuss. She survived the rejection of a husband by burrowing into the love of God. She showed me how to live with purpose through pain and all the while blessed those around her. Gwendolyn Vance Boyd Foth was the definition of "true grit."

Paul's words in Romans 8 capture it precisely:

Who shall separate us from the love of Christ? Shall trouble or hardship or persecution or famine or nakedness or danger or sword? . . . No, in all these things we are more than conquerors through him who loved us. (vv. 35, 37)

Mom was more than a survivor, as great as that is. My mother was a victor. What a legacy!

St. Francis of Assisi captures the idea of legacy-as-gift best in one riveting sentence: "Remember that when you leave this earth, you can take with you nothing that you have received . . . but only what you have given."[1]

Gwen Foth and Roy Blakeley gave me twin legacies: grit and grace. I want to live out those legacies!

Mark's Story

Neuroimaging has shown that as we age, the center of cognitive gravity tends to shift from the imaginative right brain to the logical left brain. That neurological tendency presents a grave spiritual danger: at some point, most of us stop living out of imagination and start living out of memory. Instead of creating the future, we repeat the past. Instead of living by faith, we live by logic. But it doesn't have to be that way. Dick has shown me that.

At seventy-two, Dick is dreaming bigger dreams than ever before. This book is one of them. And he's already working on his next one! Dick is also finding new ways to multiply his influence through mentoring. He recently pitched his latest brainstorm with an excitement level typically reserved for someone who's just won the lottery. It's a forty-eight-hour adventure with Dick and Ruth that includes lots of conversations about

God and life and love, Ruth's homemade apple pie à la mode, and maybe even climbing Horsetooth Mountain like Foth and I did a few years back.

As we age, one of two things happens: either memory overtakes imagination or imagination overtakes memory. Imagination is the road less traveled, but that is the path Dick Foth has chosen to travel. I may be thirty years behind him, but I'd like to follow Foth as he follows Christ. It's hard to reduce a Renaissance man down to one catchphrase, but to me, Dick Foth's legacy is this: he turns everything into an adventure. Every relationship. Every circumstance. Every day. One adventure after another!

Life is a dress rehearsal. The grand adventure awaits us when we cross the space-time continuum and enter a reality the Bible simply describes as heaven. But why not get a jump on it now?

An inheritance consists of the tangible things we leave behind. A legacy is the intangible things we leave behind. My grandparents, Elmer and Alene Johnson, left both. My grandma outlived my grandpa by nearly two decades. She survived on Social Security and a meager retirement, but somehow she managed to leave an inheritance that paid off my school loans in one fell swoop. I'm grateful for that inheritance, but more than that, I'm grateful for the legacy they left. One of my first memories is hearing my Grandpa Johnson pray for me. He had a nightly ritual of kneeling next to his bed, taking off his hearing aid, and praying for my family by name. He couldn't hear himself pray, but everybody else in the house could. My most prized possession? My grandfather's 1934 Thompson Chain-Reference Study Bible. I've never seen a more well-read, well-worn, well-lived Bible—the pages are literally taped together. The old adage is true: if someone's Bible is falling apart, their life probably isn't. I'd like to leave an inheritance for my children and grandchildren, but more importantly, I'd like to leave each of them a well-read, well-worn, well-lived Bible.

When President Franklin Delano Roosevelt died, First Lady Eleanor Roosevelt was comforted by a piece of poetry given to her by a friend:

> They are not dead who live in lives they leave behind:
> In those whom they have blessed they live a life again.[2]

That's certainly true of my pastor and my father-in-law, Bob Schmidgall.

The first time I met him, I was a thirteen-year-old kid. It was two o'clock in the morning and I was in the intensive care unit at Edward Hospital in Naperville, Illinois. When the doctors issued a code blue, my parents called the Schmidgall's home phone. We'd only been to Calvary Church a few times, but that didn't keep him from coming to the hospital in the wee hours of the morning to pray for me, no questions asked. Nearly a decade later, I would ask for his daughter's hand in marriage. My pastor became my father-in-law.

My father-in-law was one of a kind. He was a tough personality to pin down. But when you were with him, you knew this: he loved to laugh, he loved life, he loved his family, and he loved God heart, soul, mind, and strength. I have a lot of memories of Dad. I remember him doing *Chicago Tribune* crossword puzzles every single day. I remember his infamous hook shot from the free throw line. I remember him laughing till his face turned red or hot chocolate came out his nostrils. I remember going to Bulls games during the Michael Jordan era. And I remember buckling my seat belt whenever I was a passenger in the car he was driving! What I remember most, however, is the way his presence somehow made even the most mundane moments meaningful and memorable.

When he passed away from a heart attack two years into our church plant, we were blindsided. He left a larger-than-life hole in our hearts. Lora lost her dad and I lost my mentor. I felt like I needed more years with him. To soak up his wisdom. To receive his blessing. To pick his brain about raising a family and starting a church. A hundred times since then I've said to Lora, "I wonder what Dad would do" or "I wonder what Dad would think" or "I wish Dad could be here now."

Legacy is the essence of a person—their hopes, their dreams, their passions. It's the part of their personality, their character, that you want to emulate. The people who have the greatest influence on our lives create a backdrop against which we judge ourselves. My backdrop is my father-in-law. He was a visionary pastor. A servant leader. A prayer warrior.

A few years ago, I wrote a book on prayer titled *The Circle Maker* that God has blessed beyond my wildest dreams. I owe it to my father-in-law. My favorite page in that book is the dedication page: "To my father-in-law, Bob Schmidgall. The memory of you kneeling in prayer lives forever, as do your prayers."[3] I wrote *a* book on prayer. My father-in-law wrote *the* book. I've never met anyone who prayed with more consistency or intensity. He hit his knees long before sunrise. And when he laid his huge farm hands on your head to pray for you and prayed from the depths of his soul, you felt like there was no way God wasn't going to answer!

Bob Schmidgall dreamed God-sized dreams. But even as Calvary Church grew into the thousands, he never stopped putting a towel around his waist and washing feet. No dream was too big, but no task was too small. That unique combination of leadership and servanthood made him who he was. Even as his responsibilities and opportunities expanded, he remained the humble servant. I remember walking across the church campus with him one day and seeing him bend over to pick up little scraps of paper from the floor. He dropped them in the garbage can on our way out the door. The church had an entire janitorial staff. It was their job to clean up the church, but he lived out servant leadership in a tangible way every day.

When Lora was growing up, her dad would rarely drive by a stranded motorist without stopping to see if he could help them change a flat, jump a battery, or give them a lift. Lora would occasionally protest during her teen years, but it's one of those good old-fashioned kindness qualities that we now appreciate the most. I see his servant leadership in Lora when she's packing lunches for our homeless ministry on Saturday nights. I see his heart for missions in my brother-in-law, Joel Schmidgall, who serves as our executive pastor. For the record, Joel was one of Dick's aide-de-camps before coming on staff at NCC. If I closed my eyes while listening to him preach, I would swear it was my father-in-law! He also inherited his father's huge heart for missions. NCC gave $1.8 million to missions last year, and we'll take thirty-three missions trips this year. We're simply living out the legacy that has been left to us.

One of my father-in-law's idiosyncrasies that I've imported into my life is answering the phone anytime my wife or kids call. It doesn't matter who I'm with or what I'm doing; I want them to know that they are never an interruption. In little ways and big ways, my life is a reflection of his. I've asked God for the privilege of pastoring one church for life. Why? Because I saw that modeled by my father-in-law. I saw what God can accomplish if you plant yourself in one place for thirty-one years and let your roots grow deep.

A long obedience in the same direction. That's what Dad modeled day in and day out, week in and week out. He weathered the storms; he weathered conflict; he weathered the ups and downs; he weathered the successes and failures. It's amazing what you can accomplish if you keep kneeling, keep your eyes fixed on Christ, and keep on keeping on.

When my father-in-law passed away, six thousand people paid their last respects at the wake. Many of them were the people he had pastored for three decades. Some of them had never even met my father-in-law, but his radio broadcast impacted their lives. They came to honor his life and legacy. After the funeral service, a procession of cars drove to Naperville Cemetery for the graveside service. The police escort told us afterward that when the hearse pulled into the cemetery, cars where still leaving the church five miles away! That's his legacy—five miles of influence.

Our uniqueness is a gift from God. And our uniqueness is our gift we give back to God. When I stand before our heavenly Father, he won't say, "Why weren't you more like Dick Foth or Bob Schmidgall?" He'll say, "Why weren't you more like Mark Batterson?" Each of us is a one-of-a-kind original. But this I know for sure: I wouldn't be who I am without their stream of influence in my life. Elmer Johnson. Dick Foth. Bob Schmidgall. They are my cloud of witnesses. Each of them left a wide and wonderful wake for me to follow. That's legacy at it's best.

Don't Just Leave an Inheritance, Leave a Legacy

20

Two Thumbs Up

Dick's Story

Epitaph means "above the tomb." It identifies the "who" and sometimes the "what" of the person buried there. But a real epitaph is not chiseled in stone, is it? Like the law of God—it is written on people's hearts.

In May of 2013, Ruth and I sat talking in a cabin with a handful of friends in Estes Park, Colorado, two hours from our home. I am the talker in the family. Ruth, reserved and quiet, at one point indicated her wish to say something. She said, "I don't know if I can do this because my heart is pounding, but I'll try!" As an encouragement to one of our friends, she quoted a favorite poem.

Finishing, she slid back in the love seat beside me, then suddenly gasped and slumped to her left. Grabbing her shoulders, I turned her to me and looked right into the gray face of death. Her mouth and eyes were open, pupils dilated, and except for a faint rattle in her throat, she was not breathing.

She had suffered what doctors call *sudden cardiac death*, which occurs when the electrical system in the heart shorts out and the heart ceases to pump blood. Without the oxygen carried to the brain by the blood, the cortex shuts down and you are gone. In that moment, as my world caved in, I started to sob, shouting, "Ruthie, don't leave me!" Instantly, people started praying, and someone called 911.

In the blur of the following minutes, a rookie police officer ran in, dropped to his knees, and began chest compressions. Sirens wailing in the distance signaled more help on the way, and within moments paramedics were there. They cut off Ruth's clothes and, on their knees, created a working circle. I could see nothing but her bare feet. Our friends were making calls across the country. Others stood praying. The EMS team worked with a feverish calm to insert IVs and prepare the defibrillator, taking turns doing chest compressions.

I heard someone say, "Clear!" The shock lifted her heels off the floor. No pulse. The CPR count was a metronome: "One-two-three-four-five." Another shock. Nothing. I sat at the seven o'clock position to her about six feet away, stunned and weeping. Then a third shock. And someone said, "We have a pulse."

A helicopter airlifted Ruth from the ER in Estes to the Medical Center of the Rockies in Loveland. The cardiologist told us, "Here's the deal. We will take her body temperature to 92 degrees for twenty-four hours. Then we will warm her back up a half a degree an hour over twelve hours. At that time we'll cut back the sedation. That will be the first point at which we are able to tell anything. Don't expect much. Her brain and body have taken a terrific insult. She might wake up. She might wake up with brain damage. Or she might never wake up. We have no idea how much damage has been done."

Some days later we learned the statistics: 88 percent of people who experience sudden cardiac death do so alone and die on the spot. Of the other 12 percent, only one in twenty walks out of the hospital. Far fewer than that walk out without brain deficit.

The next forty hours were a dark night of the soul. Our family arrived within twenty-four hours to keep vigil. Erica, our eldest, changed her profile picture on Facebook to a picture of a lit candle. Within minutes hundreds of people around the world were posting pictures of candles. We were surrounded by light and lifted by prayer.

The kids took shifts being with me in Ruth's room. Sleep only happened at the edges. Each time I closed my eyes, I would see her death face and weep. This was the woman who had steadied me for fifty years. I told the kids, "The doctors don't know what the damage might be. But I've told God, I will take her any way I can get her." In those hours, I had never been so scared, never cried so much, and never trusted more.

At 5:00 p.m. on May 23, the doctors began the warming process. I finally dozed off around midnight. At 2:10 in the morning, a dear friend sitting up with Ruth shook me. Ruth was waking up.

Earlier that night Dr. Thomas Matthew, a cardiac surgeon, was doing his rounds and came into the ICU. I had only met him once in passing, but he said to me, with virtually no empirical data to support the statement, "Dick, I have a sense this is going to be okay." Then, to my astonishment, he asked, "May I pray for Ruth?" "Absolutely," I said. He put his hand on her inert form and in a strong voice said, "Lord God Almighty, I pray that you will heal Ruth from the top of her head to the toes of her feet." At 2:10 a.m., I was shaken awake from a fitful sleep in a chair at the head of her bed. The answer to that prayer and the thousands of others had showed up.

As I scrambled up and stood beside her bed, the nurse started testing Ruth's responses. "Ruth, open your eyes." She slowly opened her eyes.

"Look at me." She looked at him.

"Squeeze my hand." She squeezed his hand.

He said, "Wiggle your toes." Her toes moved.

"Wiggle the toes on your right foot." Just those toes moved.

He said, "Shrug your shoulders." She did.

"Give me a smile." A half-smile formed around her breathing tube.

Finally, "Give me two thumbs up!" When she did, I lost it. The quiet of the ICU was shattered by tearful praises. Ruth was coming back. The medical team used "miracle" language.

In those excruciating hours, it was clear that Ruth's epitaph was already written on my heart. It is simply and profoundly this: *She loves me.* In small and large ways, Ruth has loved me with transforming steadiness. No one but Jesus has shaped me more. I could travel to a hundred countries, chase a thousand dreams, and give a million talks, and it would be empty without her.

I saw her epitaph etched in our children's faces in the dark of the night, as they kissed her hands and face and whispered, "We love you, Mom. You are the best mom. We know that you need to rest now, but in the morning we are going to need you to wake up."

Two months after Ruth woke up, we celebrated our fiftieth anniversary with the entire clan. In a large house in the San Diego hills for a week, we lived in the pool and played and ate and laughed. Then came the first ever Foth family talent show. Kids and grandkids sang and played the piano. They did basketball tricks and lip-synched like pros. At the end, music thumping through the house, they got up and danced. We joined them in a jig of joy. It was sacred. It was a Lazarus moment. More precisely, according to a friend, it was a *Lazaruth* moment!

May 2013 is captured for Ruth and me in one word: *prayer.* And *prayer* is a mighty fine epitaph. March 19, 1872, was David

Livingstone's fifty-ninth birthday. On that day he made this entry in his journal:

> Lord, send me anywhere, only go with me. Lay any burden on me, only sustain me. Sever any ties, save the tie that binds me to thy heart. My Jesus, my King, my life, my all, I again dedicate my whole self to Thee.[1]

In that simple language we find the beginning and end of The Grand Adventure.

Mark's Story

For four decades, Amos Alonzo Stagg coached football at the University of Chicago. They were the original Monsters of the Midway, long before the Bears borrowed that moniker. My undergraduate education began at the University of Chicago, and I quickly discovered that I couldn't go too far on campus without bumping into Stagg's influence. Not only did he lead the Maroons to two national titles in 1905 and 1913, but his football legacy includes the huddle, the Statue of Liberty play, the onside kick, the T formation, the end-around, and the forward pass.[2] In other words, he practically invented football as we know it. But that isn't his true legacy. When he accepted the invitation to coach the Maroons, he gave the university president an acceptance speech of sorts, saying, "After much thought and prayer, I decided that my life can best be used for my Master's service in the position you have offered."[3] Amos Alonzo Stagg coached until the age of ninety-eight, but he didn't just coach his teams. He discipled them.

After a particularly successful season, a young reporter congratulated Stagg on a job well done. Instead of simply receiving that compliment, he coached that young reporter. In his straightforward manner, Coach Stagg said, "I won't know how good a job I did for twenty years. That's when I'll see how my boys turned out."[4]

Our legacy isn't measured by what we accomplish during our life on earth. It's measured by the lives that are changed long after we're long gone. My grandfather died when I was six, but his prayers are still being answered in my life. My father-in-law died when I was twenty-eight, but he still sets the standard. And I hope Dick Foth makes a hundred trips around the sun, but his legacy won't die when he does. It'll live on in his family, his friends, his aide-de-camps, and a pastor named Mark Batterson whom he has befriended and mentored and spiritually fathered for nearly two decades now. And now that you've read *A Trip around the Sun*, it'll live on in your life too.

What kind of legacy do you want to leave?

Don't leave it to chance. It's a choice.

Epitaphs are a powerful thing. What is said about us when we die is a window into how we lived our lives. Epitaphs reveal the innate desire each of us has within us to leave an impact on the world. Even after we have left this earth, we want to leave something of ourselves behind. We want to be remembered for something.

Ludolph van Ceulen, a Dutch mathematician who was the first to calculate pi, died at the age of seventy in 1610. He had 3.14159265358979323846264338327950 engraved on his tombstone. He wanted his proudest achievement to be known to all as he entered eternity.

Benjamin Franklin once wrote an epitaph for himself in one of his journals. It read: "The Body of B. Franklin, Printer, like the Cover of an old Book, Its Contents torn out, And stript of its Lettering and Gilding, Lies here, Food for Worms. But the Work shall not be wholly lost; For it will, as he believ'd appear once more, In a new & more perfect Edition, Corrected and

amended by the Author."[5] Ben Franklin, one of America's found-
ing fathers, was a renowned scientist, ambassador to France,
inventor, postmaster, writer, and musician. But he always considered himself a printer at heart. A true Renaissance man, he
helped usher in the age of democracy in our country. He arrived
penniless on the streets of Philadelphia as a teenager from his
hometown of Boston. Sixty-seven years later, when he died at
the age of eighty-four, twenty thousand Philadelphians turned
out to honor him.

You may not be a van Ceulen or a Franklin. You may never
achieve fifteen minutes of fame in your days here on earth.
But isn't your epitaph something you should give some serious
thought to? Epitaphs aren't something we normally discuss in
everyday conversation. Just as we avoid thinking about dying,
most of us have given little thought to the words that we want
to be remembered by. What is your passion in life? What breaks
your heart? What stirs your imagination? What are you willing
to give your life for? What do you want to leave behind when
your days here on earth are done? Sometimes asking ourselves
questions helps us reevaluate where we are. If tomorrow was
your last day on earth, would your epitaph read the way you
would want it to?

I love wandering through old cemeteries and reading the
inscriptions on tombstones. The epitaphs inspire me to live my
life for something that will outlast it. My favorite cemetery sits
right across the Potomac River from the Lincoln Memorial.
Arlington Cemetery is one of the most beautiful and reverential
spots in the nation's capital. Originally the home of Martha
Washington's grandson, George Washington Parke Custis, Arlington House was meant to be a living memorial to George
Washington. When Custis's daughter married the Commander
of the Confederate Army, Robert E. Lee, he became the caretaker
of the estate before losing it to the federal government during

the Civil War. It eventually became the final resting place for thousands of soldiers who have sacrificed their lives for the cause of freedom.

When you are walking between row upon row of simple white markers, you get the sense that you are walking on hallowed ground. The hopes and dreams of more than 400,000 servicemen and servicewomen are laid to rest across the span of Arlington's 624 acres. These lives weren't lived in vain. They were lived with a purpose, with a belief in their country and its freedom, and with a willingness to serve. There is something solemn and awesome about reading the inscriptions on the stones. It's like they speak from beyond the grave. It's a poignant reminder to live life while we're living. Simply put: *it's never too late to be who you might have been.*

There is another cemetery I like to visit. You won't find any military monuments there. No heads of state or renowned scholars. It isn't a famous cemetery, but the person who lays there is famous to me. My father-in-law, Bob Schmidgall, is buried in Naperville Cemetery, at the corner of S. Washington Street and W. Martin Ave. It's across the street from Naperville Central High School, where I spent four of the best years of my life. It's across the other street from ManorCare, the nursing home where I preached some of my first sermons. And it's down the block from where I spent much of my youth playing Little League baseball and Pop Warner football.

Etched on my father-in-law's tombstone is a simple and succinct epitaph: "Well done, good and faithful servant." Epitaphs are testimonies. They bear witness to a life well lived. My father-in-law's is a reminder that God won't say, "Well thought" or "Well said" or "Well planned." There is only one commendation: "Well done." And there is no higher commendation than that. It is the epitaph that every Christ follower wants written over their lives. Anything less than that is falling short.

It is not too late to rewrite your epitaph. It's a living document. An epitaph is not the period at the end of our life sentence. It's the prologue to our eternal story. How you live out your days on this earth will determine how you will live out your days in eternity.

A. W. Tozer once said, "Eternity won't be long enough to discover all that God is or praise him for all that he's done."[6] Eternity is adventure without end. And those who have been faithful on earth will experience even greater adventures in heaven. Did you know that astronomers estimate the existence of at least eighty billion galaxies? That's more than ten galaxies per person! It's taken all of human history to explore one small planet in one small galaxy. So I think it's safe to say we won't get bored on the other side of the space-time continuum.

Proverbs 25:2 says, "It is the glory of God to conceal a matter; to search out a matter is the glory of kings." If you can sift through the Old English, Sir Francis Bacon had a fascinating take on that verse. He said of Solomon,

> although he excelled in the glory of treasure and magnificent buildings; of shipping and navigation; of service and attendance; of fame and renown, and the like, yet he maketh no claim to any of those glories, but only to the glory of the inquisition of truth, for so he saith expressly, The glory of God is to conceal a thing, but the glory of the king is to find it out; as if, according to the innocent play of children, the Divine Majesty took delight to hide his words to the end to have them found out and as if kings could not obtain a greater honor than to be God's play-fellows in that game, considering the great commandment of wits and means whereby nothing need be hidden from them.[7]

God's playfellows.

That's what we are. Nothing less. Nothing more. We are God's playfellows in this grand game called life. And the good news, the best news, is this: the adventure never ends!

Let your epitaph be written in a way that shouts of the goodness and greatness of God. And all of the heavens will echo an eternal "Amen."

Destiny is not a mystery. Destiny is a decision.

Choose adventure.

It's Never Too Late to Be Who You Might Have Been

Conclusion

Another Day, Another Adventure

➤ Dick's Story

The frigid Atlantic wind whipped around us as we stepped off the flight deck into the wardroom of the USS *George Washington*. The captain and a group of officers greeted us warmly. Suddenly a young lieutenant stepped forward, hand extended, and said, "Great to see you again, President Foth!" I was looking into the smiling face of a former Bethany College student, the ship's chaplain. Trips around the sun sometimes reconnect you in strange ways, at strange places.

One hundred forty miles an hour is fast by any measure. It's much faster when you are approaching a pitching deck the size of a postage stamp in the Atlantic Ocean, one hundred miles off the Virginia coast. That would be a carrier landing.

Five of us had been strapped into a Grumman Greyhound 2-A, the carrier onboard delivery aircraft (COD), which is the supply workhorse for United States Navy aircraft carriers around the world. In a five-point harness enhanced by life vest, helmet, and goggles, I faced the back of the plane. On the return trip, we would be flung off the deck of the ship by a steam catapult that would take us from 0 to 180 miles an hour in 3 seconds flat.

We were guests of Admiral Vern Clark, Chief of Naval Operations. He had asked me, "Dick, ever been on an aircraft carrier?" I said, "Once, the USS *Ranger* at Alameda Naval Air Station when I was seventeen." He said, "Not that. I mean one at sea." I replied "Never!" and he said, "Let's make that happen."

The twenty-four hours on the carrier were a blur. Since the *George Washington* was on maneuvers gearing up for deployment to the Persian Gulf, everything was action: teams going over strategies, F-18s doing nonstop takeoffs and landings all night, the calibrating and recalibrating of equipment. In short, it was hundreds of United States servicemen and servicewomen going full out.

The most captivating part for me was conversations with officers and crew ranging from the Admiral of the Fleet to cooks in the kitchen and sailors repairing and testing jet engines on the fantail of the carrier. When I asked about their mission, they all knew it. They could simply and cogently state the "why" and the "what" of their purpose.

When Admiral Clark had been appointed Chief of Naval Operations by President Clinton, sixty days before the USS *Cole* was attacked in Yemen, he had articulated a clear mission to his fellow admirals: "When young men and women raise their right hands and swear to protect the Constitution of the United States from all enemies, domestic and foreign, they also pledge to obey every superior officer above them, all the way to the Commander-in-Chief. The question is, 'What do we pledge to them?'"

He answered his own question. "We pledge that we will give them the finest training and equipment available on the planet. But, most importantly, we pledge to show them that to serve is a noble thing!"

I saw that pledge fleshed out as sailors and aircrews ran to their duties. This was more than steering a true course and launching multimillion-dollar fighters into the sky. This was mission with a capital M. It was wrapped up in freedom to worship and freedom of speech. It was about freedom to assemble and opportunities around every corner. This was about ideas that would not curtail the dream or jail the adventurer.

In previous months and years I had spent many hours with Vern Clark. His father was my boss thirty-five years earlier when Ruth and I had gone to pastor in Urbana. My function in Washington, DC, allowed me to connect with Vern on a regular basis, and I came to appreciate and even imbibe his philosophy. It reflected who he was and is. It expressed respect and trust and purpose. And it was simply this: "The Lord charts our course." Sure fits a Navy man. Fits any person who desires adventure.

We had been shown to quarters and stored our things. Then we stood a long time at a rail overlooking the flight deck as fighter after fighter was catapulted into the night, afterburners glowing like twin orange eyes in the inky dark. After a bit, the chaplain turned to me and said, "President Foth, in about an hour we will be saying the evening prayer on the ship. Would you like to do that tonight?" Tradition on naval vessels includes an evening prayer that is said over the intercom about five minutes before taps at 10:00 p.m. The tradition stems from days when there was no electronic communication and ships at sea were often in danger. Prayer was front and center.

Shortly after, I stood on the bridge of that mighty ship, looking again at the flight deck that stretched the length of three football fields. I prayed with grateful heart for the protection and care of her crew—five thousand young men and women from villages and cities across America who willingly put on "the cloth of the nation" to defend our freedoms.

The times were tumultuous, as they still are. The challenges were huge, as they still are. The possibilities of catastrophe were real, as they still are. But as the prow of that giant warship sliced through the Atlantic seas in the middle of that December night, I heard again the voice of Admiral Clark: "The Lord charts our course!"

In more than seventy trips around the sun, I have come to believe that. I haven't always felt it and haven't always acted on it. But I have known it. Deep in the recesses of my soul and in my most wrenching times, I have gone there for confidence and inspiration.

There is an insightful exchange early on in John's Gospel between Jesus and a couple of John the Baptist's followers. They meet on the banks of the Jordan River. When John points out Jesus to his own group, two of them start following Jesus. In the exchange they ask, "Where are you staying?" He doesn't tell them. He only says, "Come and see!"[1]

That's the adventure. It's a "come and see" adventure. It doesn't have a day-to-day itinerary. There are no requisitions for material or supplies. There's no timeline or end date. No guarantees are extended, except His continuing presence.

Adventuring, for me, is going somewhere new, by any means, with Jesus and friends. That's why this book is an adventure. I've never done this before. Never done it before in this way. Best of all, I got to do it with Mark. For twenty years, Mark has challenged me by his infectious intensity that infuses his devotion to Jesus into his family, his ideas, his dreams, his affirmations, his scholarship, his prayers, his laughter, and his play. I am in his debt.

Mark's Story

Jonathan Goldsmith stakes claim to being "the Most Interesting Man in the World" in Dos Equis ads, but in the real world, I vote Dick Foth. His interests are infinite. He has more trivial knowledge than anyone I know, and wisdom as well. He may not be the most networked person in Washington, but I think he may be the most *diversely* networked person. He is a quintessential storyteller and joke teller. He even does a mean Indian or British accent. With Foth, it's always another day, another adventure!

Several years ago, I spent one of the most magical weeks of my life in the Galápagos Islands with my son Parker. We logged twenty-four hours on the high seas in a tiny boat, a boat that had capsized the week before our arrival. Of course, this little detail wasn't brought up until our departure!

We island-hopped the entire week, sharing the gospel with people who had never experienced the love of Jesus. Along the way, we swam with sea lions, went cliff jumping at Las Grietas, and watched pelicans dive-bomb into the ocean and come back up with breakfast in their beaks. Countless moments will be lifelong memories, but one moment encapsulates the entire trip. I found a Spanish Sprite can with four words printed across the label, and those four words became a life motto.

Otra Dia, Otra Aventura.

Translation: *Another day, another adventure.*

Sometimes, philosophy and theology are found in the strangest places. Like a 12-ounce can of Sprite. Those four words are more than a marketing pitch. They make a pretty good mission statement. That is how I want to live out my days: Another day, Another adventure.

When I turned forty, someone sent me a link to DeathClock. com. Sounds morbid, I know. But it proved to be a liberating experience. After you enter your birthdate, body mass index, and smoking status, it reveals your very own death date. You actually have four options to choose from: optimistic, pessimistic, sadistic, or normal. I chose optimistic. My death date? October 12, 2055. Of course, I'm an eternal optimist, so I think I can beat that date!

Foth once told me that when you hit your forties, you start counting down. If the averages hold, you have more life behind you than before you. Think of it as halftime. And you can make halftime adjustments. I wonder if life really starts when you start counting down. Perhaps because you want to make it count.

I would love to make one hundred trips around the sun—a century of adventures. But that isn't up to me. God has ordained all my days.[2] But as long as I'm on the clock, I want to make each day count. I want to live like it's the first day and last day of my life.

In Colossians 3:23 Paul says, "Whatever you do, work at it with all your heart, as working for the Lord, not for human masters." When he says "work at it with all your heart," he is talking about sweat equity. Blood, sweat, and tears. Leave it all on the court, so to speak. Do it like your life depends on it. And do it for the applause of nail-scarred hands!

Author Jim Collins tells a story about his wife running the Ironman in Hawaii. In the final mile, her body began to shut down. Her muscles started cramping, so she started pounding on her thighs, willing them to finish the race. It took every ounce of strength to cross the finish line. And when she did, she had nothing left in the tank. That's how I want to finish. I certainly want to pace myself and live in a way that respects the Sabbath rhythm God has put in place. I certainly need to keep a margin for creativity and compassion. But I want to give God everything I've got. I want an A for effort. I want to hear the Father say, "Well done, good and faithful servant."

My friendship with Dick Foth began twenty years ago with an invitation to the table, their Thanksgiving table. Over the years, Dick has invited me to sit at some remarkable tables, including a table in the Senate dining room. But the last table he invited me to is quintessential Foth.

One of the kingdom causes Dick has devoted his life to is Rescue:Freedom International, a nonprofit that fights human trafficking. It's run by one of Dick's former aide-de-camps, Jeremy Vallerand, and Foth serves as the chairman of the board. In classic Foth style, he has invited his friends to come along for the ride. As I sat down at the table, I had flashbacks to the Thanksgiving table in 1994. Here I was, twenty years later, and at the table were a three-star general, a former NFL MVP, a legendary missionary couple, and more than a few multimillionaires. Some impressive résumés! And then there was *me*. This thought fired across my synapses: *How'd I get here?* Well, I have a friend named Dick Foth. That's how I got there!

I love how the evening ended.

Generals and pastors, missionaries and millionaires, CEOs and MVPs, we all held hands and sang a simple chorus led by our faithful friend—Dick Foth.

> Jesus loves me, this I know,
> For the Bible tells me so.
> Little ones to Him belong.
> They are weak, but He is strong.
>
> Yes, Jesus loves me.
> Yes, Jesus loves me.
> Yes, Jesus loves me.
> The Bible tells me so.

Every adventure begins and ends there.

Acknowledgments

➤ Dick's Thoughts

Without you, Mark, this book would not be! Your leadership at every step has been huge. In writing together, I am clearly the mouse riding on the elephant. Your heart for Jesus draws me in. Your vision and generous affirmation move me to trust Jesus more deeply.

Thank you, Ruth, for more than fifty trips around the sun! For years you said, "Dick, you need to start writing." You never issued a directive, but you should have a doctorate in rhetorical questions that never let putting pen to paper get too far off the radar. Your steady love for Jesus and for me frames my whole world.

Thank you, Susanna, for the countless hours you invested in giving our ideas and words rhythm and structure. Ever since you were a little girl, you have had the writing gift. Without that gift and your contagious enthusiasm, the words in this book would still be just talk.

When Ruth and I met Mark and Lora, only one of our children was married. Now we have four married children and eleven grandchildren. Our children and their spouses—Erica and Van, Jenny and Brett, Susanna and Scott, and Chris and Traci—have cheered us on tirelessly. And when those grandkids say, "Grandpa, tell us a story!" it's the great reward.

To the congregation of Urbana Assembly in Illinois, who loved us when we were young, we have never forgotten you. Thank you to the Bethany College family for our kids' teenage years. To our colleagues in Washington, DC, these past twenty years, your understanding of Jesus has changed how we think. To the congregations of Timberline Church in Fort Collins, CO; National Community Church in DC; Willamette Christian Center in Eugene, OR; and Calvary Church in Naperville, IL— we are in your debt.

And to our Irregular Thursday Group, your unceasing interest and faithful prayers have made the last five trips around the sun meaningful and hilarious and profound.

Mark's Thoughts

I've never had more fun writing a book, and that's a testament to Dick and Susanna. Foth, you sometimes apologize for retelling stories. Let me go on record: I could hear your stories a hundred times and want to hear them once more! And Susanna, thanks for helping us find our way through the writing forest. It was no easy task.

My primary goal in writing this book was to capture Dick's stories for posterity, but I guess I've done the same with a few of mine. I hope some of these storylines become part of our family folklore. I can't imagine life without you, Lora. And Parker, Summer, and Josiah—you've made my life more adventurous than I ever imagined.

Thanks to the church I have the privilege of serving, National Community Church. I wouldn't want to be anyplace else, doing anything else. What a joy, what a journey!

I'd like to thank our agent, Esther Fedorkevich, and the entire Fedd Agency. I say it all the time: you're the best in the business. And thanks to the team at Baker who believed in this book from its very inception. I'm grateful for your friendship and partnership.

At the end of a project like this one, I think of the many people who have made a difference in my life. I'm grateful for each and every one of you. You know who you are. Your influence is infused in every word, on every page.

 From Dick and Mark

We dedicate this book to our fellow traveler and friend, Bob Rhoden. Thanks for being in our corner.

Notes

Introduction

1. Ashley Montagu quoted in Mardy Grothe, *Oxymoronica: Paradoxical Wit and Wisdom From History's Greatest Wordsmiths* (New York: Harper, 2004), 23.
2. See Matthew 18:3.
3. Mark Batterson, "Get a Life: Creating and Sustaining a Personal Life Vision," *Enrichment Journal*, Winter 2011, http://enrichmentjournal.ag.org/201101/201101_038_Get_Life.cfm.

Chapter 1 For the Love of Risk

1. Ecclesiastes 4:12 ESV.
2. William Faulkner, *Requiem for a Nun* (New York: Vintage Books, 2011), 73.
3. See Hebrews 11:8.
4. See Matthew 2:13–15.
5. See Exodus 2:1–10.

Chapter 2 Accumulate Experiences

1. Stuart Brown with Christopher Vaughan, *Play: How It Shapes the Brain, Opens the Imagination, and Invigorates the Soul* (New York: Avery, 2009), 72–73.
2. Luke 5:29–32.

3. Philippians 3:10–11.
4. Arthur Gordon, *A Touch of Wonder* (Old Tappan, NJ: Fleming H. Revell, 1974), 181.
5. Ibid., 182.
6. Ibid.
7. If you haven't read *Moment Maker* by my friend Carlos Whitaker, you need to. He and his family also happened to be at Bob Goff's that same weekend.

Chapter 3 The Original Adventure

1. Acts 17:22–23.
2. Quoted in Rosamond Kent Sprague, *A Matter of Eternity: Selections from the Writings of Dorothy L. Sayers* (Grand Rapids: Eerdmans, 1973), 16.
3. See Matthew 20:16.
4. Matthew 16:16.

Chapter 4 The Preposition That Will Change Your Life

1. Mark 3:13–15.
2. Genesis 2:18.
3. Matthew 28:20.
4. Rick Warren, *The Purpose Driven Life* (Grand Rapids: Zondervan, 2002), 17.
5. Matthew 28:20.

Chapter 5 Who Is More Important Than What

1. Stephen E. Ambrose, *Band of Brothers: E Company, 506th Regiment, 101st Airborne from Normandy to Hitler's Eagle's Nest* (New York: Simon and Schuster, 1992), 109.
2. Ibid., 44.
3. John 15:12–15.
4. William Butler Yeats, "The Municipal Gallery Revisited," lines 55–56, in *New Poems* (1938).
5. Daniel Goleman, *Emotional Intelligence* (New York: Bantam Books, 2005), 34.
6. See their amazing products at http://www.colonellittleton.com.

Chapter 6 Stepping Stones

1. You can learn more about Rich on his website, richsride.org, and read about his bike ride at "Rich Dixon: Hope Changes What's Possible," Convoy of Hope, November 5, 2013, http://www.convoyofhope.org/advocacy/rich-dixon/.
2. Matthew 16:24 NLT.
3. Romans 10:10–11.
4. "Jim Elliot Quote," Billy Graham Center, Wheaton College, 2012, www2.wheaton.edu/bgc/archives/faq/20.htm.
5. Psalm 127:1 ESV.
6. Boris Schlossberg, "Fail Hard and Fail Often," *BK Forex*, November 27, 2011, http://www.bkforex.com/boris-schlossberg/fail-hard-and-fail-often/.
7. Thomas Edison, Brainy Quote, http://www.brainyquote.com/quotes/quotes/t/thomasaed104931.html.
8. Abraham Lincoln, Brainy Quote, http://www.brainyquote.com/quotes/quotes/a/abrahamlin121354.html.
9. Thanks to Eugene H. Peterson for this sentiment. See his book by the same title, *A Long Obedience in the Same Direction: Discipleship in an Instant Society* (Downers Grove, IL: InterVarsity, 2000).
10. See Malcolm Gladwell, *Outliers: The Story of Success* (New York: Little, Brown, 2008), chapter 2.

Chapter 7 Shared Goals

1. Quoted in Edmund Blair Bolles, *Einstein Defiant: Genius Versus Genius in the Quantum Revolution* (Washington, DC: Joseph Henry Press, 2004), 141.
2. See Matthew 6:33.
3. Acts 20:35.
4. See Hebrews 11:1.

Chapter 8 The Locus of Love

1. John 8:7.

Chapter 9 Invaluable and Irreplaceable

1. 1 John 3:1 NIV.
2. Luisa Kroll, "Inside The 2014 Forbes Billionaires List: Facts And Figures," March 3, 2014, *Forbes*, http://www.forbes.com/sites/luisakroll/2014/03/03/inside-the-2014-forbes-billionaires-list-facts-and-figures/.
3. Luke 15:1–7.
4. Matthew 3:17 NKJV.

Chapter 10 Holy and Happy

1. Mark 10:6–8.

Chapter 11 Playing for Keeps

1. 2 Timothy 1:5.

2. Parker has coauthored with me *The Circle Maker Student Edition, All In Student Edition,* and *The Grave Robber Student Edition.*

Chapter 12 Never a Dull Moment

1. Matthew 25:35–36, 40, emphasis added.

2. Stephen R. Covey, A. Roger Merrill, and Rebecca R. Merrill, *First Things First* (New York: Simon & Schuster, 1994), 32.

3. Mark 12:30.

4. Quoted in Pam Rosewell Moore, *Life Lessons from the Hiding Place: Discovering the Heart of Corrie ten Boom* (Grand Rapids: Chosen, 2004), 38.

Chapter 13 The Five-and-a-Half-Inch World between Your Ears

1. See Proverbs 23:7 KJV.

2. Hugh Downs, "Georgia Centenarian Study," *20/20* (television program), produced by Fred Peabody, edited by Bud Proctor, 1992. Clip available online at https://www.you tube.com/watch?v=o_uh7rpYUig (accessed October 6, 2014).

3. See Philippians 3.

4. Aldous Huxley, *Texts and Pretexts* (London: Chatto & Windus, 1932), 5.

5. See Psalm 90:12.

Chapter 14 Books with Skin Covers

1. Ralph Waldo Emerson quoted in Dale Carnegie, *How to Win Friends and Influence People* (New York: Pocket Books, 1981), 28.

2. Ecclesiastes 4:9.

3. Harry Truman quoted in Hugh Sidey, "The Presidency: Will These Mud Crawlers Learn to Fly?" *Time,* November 7, 1988.

Chapter 15 Learn as If You'll Live Forever

1. Leonardo Da Vinci quoted in Michael J. Gelb, *How to Think Like Leonardo da Vinci: Seven Steps to Genius Every Day* (New York: Bantam Dell, 2004).

2. See 2 Corinthians 10:5.

3. Ronald Clark, *Einstein: The Life and Times* (New York: Bloomsbury, 1972).

4. Quoted in Max Jammer, *Einstein and Religion: Physics and Theology* (Princeton, NJ: Princeton University Press, 1999), 120.

5. The exact quote is, "Every now and then a man's mind is stretched by a new idea or sensation, and never shrinks back to its former dimensions." From Oliver Wendell Holmes, *The Autocrat of the Breakfast-Table* (Boston: James R. Osgood and Co., 1873); online at Project Gutenberg, http://www.gutenberg.org/ebooks/751.

6. Andy Stanley, *Next Generation Leader: Five Essentials for Those Who Will Shape the Future* (Colorado Springs: Multnomah, 2003), 93.

7. Ecclesiastes 11:1 NKJV.

Chapter 16 Success Is Succession

1. Margery Williams, illustrated by Michael Hague, *The Velveteen Rabbit* (New York: Henry Holt, 1983), 4–5.

2. Mitch Albom, *Tuesdays with Morrie* (New York: Random House, 1997), 118, 120–21.

Chapter 17 Reverse Mentoring

1. John 1:12 KJV.
2. Matthew 18:3.
3. See Proverbs 22:6.

Chapter 18 Fully Alive

1. C. S. Lewis, *Mere Christianity* (New York: HarperCollins, 2001), 134.
2. Philippians 3:14.
3. Tony Campolo, "If I Should Wake before I Die," *30 Good Minutes* (television broadcast), Chicago Sunday Evening Club, Program 3627, first broadcast April 25, 1993, transcription online at http://www.csec.org/ind ex.php/archives/23-member-archives /737-tony-campolo-program-3627.
4. Psalm 90:12.
5. John Wooden and Steve Jamison, *The Wisdom of Wooden* (McGraw Hill, 2010), 3.
6. See Lamentations 3:23.
7. Blaise Pascal quoted in *Forty Thousand Quotations: Prose and Poetical*, comp. by Charles Noel Douglas (New York: Halcyon House, 1917; Bartleby.com, 2012); online at http:// www.bartleby.com/348/authors/408 .html.
8. See Ephesians 5:16.

Chapter 19 Lineage and Legacy

1. St. Francis of Assisi quoted in Richard G. Capen Jr., *Empowered by Faith: Experiencing God's Love Every Day* (Grand Rapids: Zondervan, 2006), chapter 7.
2. Eleanor Roosevelt, "My Day by Eleanor Roosevelt," April 26, 1945, The Eleanor Roosevelt Papers Project, http://www.gwu.edu/~erpapers/my day/displaydoc.cfm?_y=1945&_f=md 000008.
3. Mark Batterson, *The Circle Maker: Praying Circles around Your Biggest Dreams and Greatest Fears* (Grand Rapids: Zondervan, 2011), 5.

Chapter 20 Two Thumbs Up

1. John Dreisbach, "Missionary Biographies: David Livingstone," Gospel Fellowship Association, http:// www.gfamissions.org/missionary-bio graphies/livingstone-david-1813-18 73.html (accessed June 7, 2014).
2. "Amos Alanzo Stagg," Wikipedia, http://en.wikipedia.org/wiki/Am os_Alonzo_Stagg. Modified November 18, 2014.
3. Collin Hansen, "Football's Pious Pioneer," ChristianHistory.net, August 8, 2008, http://www.christian itytoday.com/ch/news/2005/jan14.ht ml?start=2.
4. John Wooden and Steve Jamison, *The Wisdom of Wooden* (New York: McGraw Hill, 2010), 19.
5. J. A. Lemay, *The Life of Benjamin Franklin, Volume 1: Journalist, 1706–1730* (Philadelphia: University of Pennsylvania Press, 2013), 321.
6. A. W. Tozer, *The Pursuit of God* (Camp Hill, PA: Christian Publications, 1982), 25.
7. Quoted in William Henry Churcher, *The Mystery of Shakespeare Revealed* (1886; repr. London: Forgotten Books, 2013), 36–7.

Conclusion

1. See John 1:35–39.
2. See Psalm 139:16.

Mark Batterson is the *New York Times* bestselling author of *The Circle Maker* and *The Grave Robber*. The lead pastor of National Community Church in Washington, DC, Mark has a doctor of ministry degree from Regent University and lives on Capitol Hill with his wife, Lora, and their three children.

Richard Foth is the father of four and grandfather of eleven. In his roles as a pastor, college president, and conference speaker, he is best known as a storyteller who believes that God's story and our stories touch the world. He holds a DMin from Gordon-Conwell Theological Seminary. He and his wife, Ruth, live in Colorado.

Susanna Foth Aughtmon is the author of *All I Need Is Jesus and a Good Pair of Jeans* and *My Bangs Look Good and Other Lies I Tell Myself*. After pursuing various careers, including her own interior decorating business, she decided to stay home as a full-time mom. A pastor's wife and mother of three, Susanna assists her husband, Scott, in various ministries at the church they planted in California.

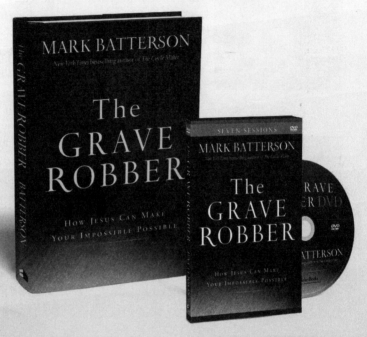